BOOK PRAISE

Ethan is one very blessed young man! Fortunately, we can all share in the wisdom and practical insight that his grandfather has shared with him in these pages. Read it. Share it. Live it.

> Matthew Kelly, New York Times
> bestselling author, *The Rhythm of Life*
> and *The Dream Manager*

A delightful, insightful, one-of-a-kind handbook on how to be great parents and grandparents. Looking for common ground with your children and grandchildren? This is the book for you.

> Fr. Mike Lydon
> Pastor
> St. Thomas Aquinas Catholic Church
> New Port Richey, FL

Tom's living legacy to our organization is the *Spirit of Excellence* program that enriches the lives of our staff members even today. Don't miss an opportunity to read *Letters to Ethan*. It's more than a book; it's an invitation to embrace what really matters in life.

Catherine A. Hanover
Vice President, Government Affairs
St. Elizabeth Medical Center
Utica, NY

I discovered Tom's purpose and passion for life when we collaborated on a customer service training initiative for the Tampa Bay Rays MLB team several years ago. His latest book, *Letters to Ethan,* will enrich your perspective on parenting and grandparenting while refocusing your personal priorities.

José Tavarez
President & CEO
Total Sports Group, LLC
Tampa, FL

Every grandparent and parent will gain wisdom and insight from this remarkable book.

Sister Jean Liston, GNSH
Director of Pastoral Services
Church of St. Andrew
Newtown, PA

Letters To Ethan
A Grandfather's Legacy of Life & Love

LETTERS TO ETHAN

A GRANDFATHER'S LEGACY OF LIFE & LOVE

TOM McQUEEN

Seraphina Press
Minneapolis, MN

SERAPHINA
PRESS

Seraphina Press

212 3rd Avenue North, Suite 290

Minneapolis, MN 55401

612.455.2293

www.SeraphinaPress.com

ISBN - 978-0-9841965-9-3

ISBN - 0-9841965-9-5

LCCN - 2010933101

Cover Design by Robert Aulicino, www.aulicinodesign.com

Typeset by Sophie Chi

Printed in the United States of America

Contents

ACKNOWLEDGEMENTS

I ACKNOWLEDGE JESUS CHRIST as my Lord and Savior and thank Him for the gift of my life.

While I never knew my paternal grandparents, I want to thank them for teaching my father the meaning of sacrifice for one's family.

And I want to thank my maternal grandparents, Edward and Anna Lenk, for living the true meaning of being grandparents when I was growing up with them in our home in Yorkville, New York.

Finally, I want to acknowledge the ministers of all faiths who labor to bring the message of God's love to their people.

DEDICATION

To my grandson, Ethan McQueen.
I love you, Ethan, with all of my heart.

FOREWORD

*I*F YOU COULD READ just one book with the potential to positively impact the lives of your children and grandchildren, this is the book.

Letters to Ethan will make you laugh one minute and cry the next. Most importantly, Tom McQueen's emotionally riveting letters to his grandson offer parents and grandparents incredibly powerful life lessons that their kids and grandkids can use as guideposts for their ongoing growth and development.

What we give to our children and grandchildren in this life pales in comparison to the legacy that we can leave for their future. And in this timely and wonderfully insightful personal testimony, Tom defines for us the essence of a Christian legacy and beautifully links that legacy to our heritage as children of God.

While you'll be able to read this book in a short time, you'll want to keep it as a reference for a lifetime. Each letter to Ethan is packed with practical wisdom that parents and grandparents can employ to coach and counsel their children who are discovering their purpose and meaning in life.

With degrees in philosophy, theology, and over twenty-five years experience as a marriage and family therapist, Tom McQueen challenges us to embrace our vocations as the leaders of our families while becoming a hope and a help to the children God has entrusted to our care.

Read this book. Enjoy this book. Use this book. And your children will be richly blessed with a never-ending legacy.

Rudy Ruettiger
Inspiration for the movie *Rudy*

PREFACE

I REMEMBER THE DAY, the time, and the place. I remember the restaurant and where I was sitting. Joe and Alison told my wife and me that there was something they wanted to share with us. Not long after we arrived and ordered lunch it was with little fanfare my son announced, "We want to tell you that Alison's pregnant and we're going to have a baby."

For a few seconds and maybe longer than that, I didn't know how to react. I wasn't sure whether to laugh, cry, or stand up on the table and jump for joy. Reflecting back on that moment, there were a million thoughts racing through my mind all at once, paralyzing the expression of any emotion. I just sat there for what seemed like an eternity and thought, "I'm going to be a grandfather."

After we left the restaurant, and in the subsequent evening hours, I was excited about the responsibility of being a grandparent and I prayed that I would have the wisdom and the strength to fulfill my role in a way that would create a legacy for this precious gift from God.

When Ethan was born on that November day, I made him a promise in my heart that I would become the very best grandfather that I was capable of becoming and that I would share with him those lessons that had shaped my journey here on earth with the hope that he would someday find those insights meaningful in his own life.

And while this book is a partial fulfillment of that promise, it's my hope that others will also benefit from the mistakes and the miracles that have taught me the real purpose for living. Enjoy!

"Life is a promise. Fulfill it."

Mother Teresa

𝒟EAR ETHAN:

In my first letter I want to share with you the most important lesson that I have ever learned in my life. It's a lesson I hope you'll always remember and one that I pray will guide you in the years to come.

When I was in college studying theology and psychology, one of the priests we all admired and respected would give us a quiz every Friday on the material he taught us during the week. His quizzes were always the same, twenty-five questions, four points each, and so easy that just about everyone in our class always earned an "A."

So on the Friday before Thanksgiving vacation it was no surprise when Father Donatus distributed probably the easiest quiz of the semester to his twenty students. As I looked around the room I could see my fellow classmates zipping through the answers with big smiles on their faces knowing full well that they most likely achieved another high grade for their effort.

Today, however, there would be an unexpected surprise. When the first student brought his paper forward, Father

1

Donatus said that on this day there would be a "Part 2" to the quiz that would be worth fifty of the possible one hundred points. As he distributed to each student the paper containing the second half of the examination, there were looks of puzzlement and bewilderment as they returned to their seats. And when I received my paper, I understood their visible frustration.

The second section of the quiz comprised one question worth fifty points. That was bad enough. What made it worse was the question itself: "Write down the first name of the woman who cleans our school." Huh? "Write down the first name of the woman who cleans our school." What the heck did that have to do with theology or psychology?

Well, our classroom was located in a pretty small education building and on many occasions I had seen the woman whose name was worth fifty points. I passed her coming out of the cleaning closet or near the bathrooms with her mop and pail, and several times on the stairwell. The problem was that I didn't know her first name and I didn't want to hazard a guess for fear of looking really stupid. I left the question blank.

I couldn't begin to tell you, Ethan, how mad I was at Father Donatus for asking what I thought was really an unfair question that had nothing to do with the subject matter that we were studying. It made no sense. I already knew that I failed before I even had my paper graded.

When class convened on the following Monday, Father Donatus returned our quizzes and no one in the class passed. Several of us earned fifty points and had a huge, bright red

"F" in the center of each paper. No one knew the first name of the woman who cleaned our school.

When we asked Father Donatus why knowing that information was important in the field of psychology and theology, I'll never forget his answer. He was sitting at his desk, took off his glasses and paused for a moment. Then he began quietly and succinctly, "Gentlemen ... you can read all of the books and study all of the principles of religion and behavioral science and become very smart scholars, even recognized in your chosen field of endeavor. But none of that really matters ... because the single most important purpose for living is to know people, to engage people, and to uplift people."

In my life's journey to date, I never learned a more important lesson. Think about it, Ethan. If the majority of people living today took that lesson to heart and acted accordingly, what a magnificent world it would be for everyone.

And I was gently reminded of the importance of knowing people, engaging them, and uplifting them when you were born. I was standing in your Mom's hospital room as you rested in her arms, thinking about what was written in the book of the prophet Isaiah, "Before you were born, I knew you. I called you by name." Yes, of the people in that hospital room on November 2, you were the one who had been most recently in God's company. He knew you. He called you by name. And He sent you into this world created in His image and likeness.

I made a commitment that day to know you, engage you,

and uplift you as your grandfather. What I never realized is just how much you would do the same for me, for your parents, and even for complete strangers in your very first year of life.

Until I experienced the joy of watching you grow and develop in those early months, I forgot what I had learned when your Dad was born, that "unless you become like a little child, you will never enter the kingdom of heaven."

Without question, you mirrored that sense of wonder and amazement that makes life a miracle. Your grandmother and I would take you to the mall and watch you discover everything from the escalators to the Disney store to the ice skating rink. Your eyes told the story of your heart. You were fearless, bounced back from falls and frustrations, and interacted with people from all walks of life with a wave and a smile. Even Santa Claus wasn't frightening as you slapped him a high five and returned to visit him several times during the Christmas season.

All of the wonderful qualities that I saw in you as a child I'm sad to say that I rarely see in adults today and even in myself on more occasions than I care to admit. Life is curious. In our youngest years we seem to reflect most closely those attributes of life that God wants us to employ to make the world a better place. As we grow older and embrace the demands of family and career, our "busyness" seems to lure us away from that basic mission articulated so poignantly by Father Donatus. We invest our energy searching for an answer to the question, "What is it that I really want?" Finally, as the reality of our mortality creeps

4

into our consciousness on a more frequent basis, thoughts of our relationship to God hopefully prompt a new question that begs an answer, "What is wanted of me?"

Ethan, I'm not suggesting that the most important lesson in my life become the most important lesson in yours. Sure, I hope that what I have learned provides some guidance for your life's journey, as I said earlier, but you have to learn your own lessons, make your own decisions, and experience life on your terms. What I do know for certain, though, is that whatever effort you put into knowing, engaging, and uplifting people throughout your life, it will come back to you a hundredfold in the quality of your personal and professional relationships.

Finally, Ethan, I want you to know that Eleanor was her name ... the woman who cleaned my school. She was widowed, had five children, and cleaned our education building on campus to make ends meet. When she died unexpectedly, I was fortunate to be able to attend the Mass of Resurrection at her church, meet each one of her children, and thank them for the impact that their mother had on my life.

I love you, Ethan.
Grandpa

"Faith is knowledge within the heart,
beyond the reach of proof."

Kahil Gibran

EAR ETHAN:

On the most lonely and desperately cold mornings in the middle of winter in Yorkville, New York, your great-grandmother, Marie, would gently awaken me from my sleep telling me that it was time to rise and shine and go to Sacred Heart Catholic Church to serve the 7 o'clock morning Mass as an altar boy.

After I put on my heavy coat, scarf, hat, and boots, I would step down from our porch and trudge through the fresh snow that had fallen throughout the night. Inevitably, the neighborhood's mean German shepherd, Max (who I think knew the Mass schedule), would be lurking for me in an alley about half-way along my four-block walk to church and took great delight in chasing me, terrorizing my ten-year-old mind.

The same handful of parishioners would faithfully be in attendance for the Latin Mass each time that it was my duty to serve for the week so I assumed that they were present on most mornings. I often wondered why they sat there in the front of church, mostly older people, listening to a language that they didn't understand and to a sermon in English that might as well have been in Latin, judging by their blank stares and nodding heads.

Growing up in Catholic schools and being taught by the Sisters of St. Joseph and the Xaverian Brothers, you can imagine that God was a frequent subject of instruction and discussion. I learned the Baltimore Catechism, didn't eat meat on Fridays during Lent, went to Confession and expressed sorrow for my sins, received absolution from a priest that I couldn't see in the confessional box, and then performed the penance that he gave me to express remorse and sorrow for my transgressions.

I was a member of the Catholic faith and proud of it. It's the faith that I learned from my parents, a faith that was nurtured by my Catholic education, a faith that I embrace today, and a faith that I shared to the best of my ability with your Dad.

But as I grew older, I began to understand that being a "member of the Catholic faith" wasn't enough. What I really needed was to build my faith in God. The loving but judgmental God of my youth needed a transformation. I wanted something that I didn't have when I was a kid. I wanted and needed a personal, one-to-one, man-to-man best friendship with the God who made me.

The weird thing is that with all of that Catholic education, we didn't seem to pay much attention to what Jesus said and did. Oh, we learned about Him in books, articles, and in class, but compared to other religions, the

Bible really didn't seem to be the focal point of my Catholic instruction.

However, as an adult, the Bible became the primary resource that led me to a deeper and more fulfilling relationship with God, especially during my studies in the seminary and for a short time as a Roman Catholic priest.

Some time ago it was fashionable to wear a bracelet with the inscription WWJD (What Would Jesus Do?). That was the fundamental question I asked myself as I grasped for a deeper understanding of what it meant to lead a responsible life and to develop that deep bond that I sought with my Creator.

During my adult years and to this very day, the personal relationship and friendship that I've developed with God is founded upon some basic understandings of faith that I want to share with you.

Based upon my life's learning and experience, Ethan, I believe that there is, in fact, a God who created us and loves us deeply. I didn't need a bachelor's degree in philosophy or a master's degree in divinity to convince me that if we look close enough at life, we will see that we are all a part of God's plan to build the Kingdom of Heaven, a place where we will live for eternity and in complete ecstasy when we die, in the presence of God, and in harmony with all of those who have gone before us and have chosen to be a part of that Kingdom. Because God gives each of His children an intellect, emotions, and a will, those gifts make everlasting happiness a choice that we make by the way that we elect to live our lives.

And so you're probably wondering, *How do we get to experience the joy of everlasting life? What are those choices that we need to make?* Well, in summarizing all of the words that have ever been written on the subject, it all boils down to the two great commandments that Jesus taught us: "You shall love the Lord your God with all your heart, and with all your soul, and with all of your mind." This is the great and first commandment. And the second is like it, "You shall love your neighbor as yourself." When we make the choice to live our lives by these two commandments, everlasting happiness is our reward in heaven when we die.

Loving God and loving our neighbor isn't always easy. We live in an imperfect world. People hurt people, sometimes violently, often times subtly. In addition, sometimes love's strength taken to the extreme becomes a weakness and we can actually love too much—to the point of causing helplessness in the lives of those that we are actually trying to help.

Of the two great commandments, that second one was the most difficult to keep when I was growing up. As you work your way through elementary and high school you're going to encounter some genuinely mean people. Kids can be cruel to one another and, believe it or not, sometimes their parents can be even worse. So "to love your neighbor as yourself" was always challenging for me especially when I wanted to punch someone's lights out. But somehow, with God's help and the guidance of my parents, I learned how to focus on my own goals while leaving the nasty stuff to those who couldn't control their emotions, let alone their lives.

So Ethan, I can't urge you enough to develop a friendship with God and make your faith in Him an integral part of the fabric of your life. Believe in God. Trust in Him. Even in the most difficult of times, know that God never leaves your side and that He always gives you the strength to manage life's most difficult and trying circumstances.

Moreover, God wants you to be happy. He wants you to use those three incredibly powerful gifts that He has given to you (your intellect, emotions, and will) to become the person that you're capable of becoming and to achieve your full potential as a human being.

If it all seems overwhelming as the years go by, I hope that you'll remember this short poem from an unknown author, which has provided me with a simple, daily purpose for my life each and every day:

God said, "Let's build a better world," and I said,
"How? The world is such a cold, dark place
and so complicated now,
And I'm so afraid that there's nothing I can do."
God, in all His wisdom said,
"Just build a better you."

I love you, Ethan.
Grandpa

> "When a man becomes a fireman his greatest
> act of bravery has been accomplished.
> What he does after that is all in the line of work."
>
> Edward F. Croker, Chief,
> FDNY, 1899-1911

EAR ETHAN:

I hope that you never have a teacher like Sister John Loretto. She was my fourth grade nightmare at Sacred Heart School and earned the nickname "Jungle John" for her foul disposition and penchant for sending her students to afternoon detention for the slightest behavioral infraction during class.

On the brighter side, Sister John also had a passion for telling us stories about the heroes of our Catholic faith and how their acts of courage contributed to the betterment of society. She would encourage each one of us to adopt a role model and make an effort to be like them in building a better world.

All of the stories were interesting but most of my buddies were more concerned about sports "heroes" like Mickey Mantle of the New York Yankees, Bobby Orr of the Boston Bruins, and the violent world of New York Giants linebacker, Sam Huff. So Sister John would grumble and grunt up and down the aisles of her classroom when she felt that the sports page was more of a focal point of discussion than the "Lives of Saints" anthology that she insisted we read during library time.

Maybe I should have paid a little more attention to Sister John in those days, Ethan, because it took me longer than I would have hoped, now that I reflect back on my childhood, to understand the difference between behaving admirably, courageously, and heroically.

Most often the men and women who wear the "hero" label in our world would never attribute that designation to themselves. When I was a kid, Mickey Mantle, Bobby Orr, and Sam Huff were unquestionably great athletes but certainly not heroes if we're talking about people who had a positive and meaningful impact upon the human condition. But were there good examples and role models to follow in the world of sports? Yes, there were many admirable and courageous stories.

I remember Wilma Rudolph when I was thirteen years old competing in the 1960 summer Olympics in Rome, Italy. Nicknamed "The Tornado" for her blazing speed, she became the first woman to win three gold medals in a single Olympic track and field competition despite running on a sprained ankle. She was, at that time, the fastest woman in the world. And while her athletic accomplishments were extraordinary, her life story was even more amazing.

Born prematurely at 4.5 pounds and to a family of nineteen siblings, Wilma Rudolph contracted infantile paralysis from the poliovirus when she was very young. Because of the virus she had to wear a brace on her left leg, which resulted in her leg being twisted. By the time she reached adolescence, she had also survived scarlet fever, whooping cough, chicken pox, and measles.

While her story paints the picture of an admirable and courageous woman who still serves today as a role model for any human being facing seemingly insurmountable obstacles, Wilma Rudolph, if she were alive today, would tell you that she's no hero.

And then there is the powerful and poignant saga of the first African-American baseball player to ever play in the major leagues, Jackie Robinson. Seeking to overcome sixty years of segregation, it was seldom easy for this gifted athlete. He endured racial slurs, being spit on and spiked by the cleats of opposing players when they would slide into a base. During a game on April 22, 1947, between the Dodgers and the Philadelphia Phillies, Phillies players called Robinson a "nigger" from their dugout and yelled that he should "go back to the cotton fields."

Jackie Robinson never abandoned his dream and after a successful ten-year career with the Brooklyn Dodgers, he became the first African-American elected to the baseball Hall of Fame in Cooperstown, New York. Mr. Robinson's reaction to all of the abuse and unpleasant confrontations he endured as he pursued his dream can be best summed up in his own words, "I'm not concerned with your liking or disliking me ... all I ask is that you respect me as a human being."

And much like Wilma Rudolph, while Jackie Robinson's story is admirable and courageous, it's not the story of a hero.

Ethan, in my lifetime, I witnessed the ultimate act of true heroism on September 11, 2001, when the United States was attacked by terrorists who commandeered three commercial airplanes and flew two of them into the World Trade Center in New York City.

On that day 343 firefighters lost their lives as they attempted to rescue those who were stranded inside the Twin Towers. As he tried to escape the 78th floor of 1 World Trade Center that day, salesman David Frank recalled the scene, "They [the firefighters] were perspiring profusely, exhausted ... and they had to go all the way to the 90s—straight into hell. This was not lost on the crowd. We all broke out into applause at one point. It was a wonderful moment."

Louis G. Lesce, making an effort to escape the 86th floor of the first tower struck, had another observation, "One fireman stopped to take a breath, and we looked each other in the eye. He was going to a place where I was damn well trying to get out of. "I looked at him thinking, *What are you doing this for?* He looked at me like he knew very well: *This is my job.*"

When Jesus Christ taught us that "greater love has no one than this, that he lay down his life for his friends" there could not have been a better description of true heroism. And on that fateful September 11 day, 343 heroes answered the call when tragedy shocked the citizens of New York

City and brought tears to the face of our nation.

Whether it be a firefighter, police officer, or soldier in the line of duty, or average citizens who place their lives in harm's way to help another human being, all true heroes have one thing in common. They all want to do the right thing. Heroes value the sacredness of humanity and will sacrifice their lives to preserve the life, dignity, and freedom of their brothers and sisters.

You're so blessed because you live in a home with two heroes. When your Dad leaves for the firehouse, he's putting his life on the line for others each and every shift. And when your Mom served as an Airman in Iraq, she took the ultimate risk for our country.

As you grow up, I know with that kind of example you'll try to do the right thing. It's in your blood and it will certainly be a part of your education and training. But most of all, I always want you to remember that you're my hero.

I love you, Ethan.
Grandpa

*D*EAR ETHAN:

It's Christmas Eve and I'm sitting here alone in our living
room. Just a few short hours ago you were here experiencing
the fun and excitement that a fourteen-month-old feels when
he sees a tree adorned with lights and colorfully wrapped
gifts, without even being able to fully comprehend the
reason for this joyous holiday.

What I want you to know is that every day that your
grandmother and I get to see you it's like celebrating
Christmas all over again. There's no doubt in my mind that
God had a sparkle in His eye when He sent you into the
world. Christmas presents are always nice to receive but,
honestly, they pale in comparison to your presence in our
lives on a daily basis.

As I've gotten older, Ethan, the commercialization of Christmas has made me very sad. The reason that God sent his son, Jesus Christ, to be born in a manger in Bethlehem on a cold winter's night is often lost today amid merchants scurrying for additional seasonal sales and customers hurrying to find that last-minute gift to put under the tree.

Some people will read the Christmas message of President Calvin Coolidge that "there will be born in us a Savior" and they will be shocked that the president of the United States would make such an assertion. Nevertheless, Ethan, despite those who contend that we were not founded as a Christian nation, the facts state otherwise.

Speaking at the Constitutional Convention, Benjamin Franklin said, "God governs in the affairs of men. And if a sparrow cannot fall to the ground without His notice, is it possible that an empire can rise without His aid?" Furthermore, in 1892 the Supreme Court of the United States wrote, "No purpose of action against religion can be imputed to any legislation, state or national, because this is a religious people. ... This is a Christian nation." The court cited eighty-seven additional precedents (prior actions, rulings, and words) concluding that we are indeed a Christian nation.

Finally, in a letter that Thomas Jefferson wrote to the Baptists of Danbury, Connecticut, (from which we derive the term "separation of Church and State") he was quite explicit in stating that the wall of separation was to insure that government would never interfere with religious activities because religious freedom came from God, not from government.

I don't need any more convincing, Ethan, that the intent of our forefathers was to acknowledge and affirm our character as a Christian nation. Hopefully, as you grow in your faith and with the guidance of your Mom and Dad, you will realize that each year you celebrate Christmas with your family you are also celebrating it with your family of fellow Americans, the family of God.

When I was much younger and at a point in my life when I was wondering what the future had in store for me, I remember receiving a Christmas card from an old friend. I was feeling a little sorry for myself in those days and the message of "One Solitary Life" touched my heart and soul. Without even realizing it, my friend sent me one of the best Christmas gifts that I had ever received.

And so for this Christmas and hopefully many in the future, I'll pray that you come to know the power of one solitary life. No matter what the situation, no matter what circumstances you encounter, because you were created in God's image and likeness, you have the ability to make a positive difference in this world. You have the ability to reach out to your family, friends, and even complete strangers to touch their lives in a meaningful way.

On that very first Christmas, the birth of Jesus Christ brought light to the world and hope to those who awaited the birth of the Savior. Every time you let your light shine and brighten the lives of those around you, that spirit of

Christmas renews its presence in our world as we become a hope and a help to one another.

One Solitary Life

(Adapted from an essay by Dr. James Allan Francis, 1926)

He was born in an obscure village
The child of a peasant woman.
He grew up in another obscure village
Where he worked in a carpenter shop
Until he was thirty.

He never wrote a book.
He never held an office.
He never went to college.
He never visited a big city.
He never travelled more than two hundred miles
From the place where he was born.
He did none of the things
Usually associated with greatness.
He had no credentials but himself.

He was only thirty three.
His friends ran away.
One of them denied him.
He was turned over to his enemies
And went through the mockery of a trial.
He was nailed to a cross between two thieves.

While dying, his executioners gambled for his clothing,
The only property he had on earth.
When he was dead
He was laid in a borrowed grave
Through the pity of a friend.

Nineteen centuries have come and gone
And today Jesus is the central figure of the human race
And the leader of mankind's progress.
All the armies that have ever marched,
All the navies that have ever sailed,
All the parliaments that have ever sat,
All the kings that ever reigned put together
Have not affected the life of mankind on earth
As powerfully as that one solitary life.

Merry Christmas, Ethan! I love you.
Grandpa

"It is only with the heart that one can see rightly; what is essential is invisible to the eye."

Antoine de Saint-Exupery

EAR ETHAN:

I grew up in a modest two-story flat in a small community in upstate New York and my grandparents lived on the top floor. Running up the stairs to visit them, I would always see the one plaque that hung outside of their door. Until I left home for college, I would read the words many times and wonder what they meant for me. The plaque said: I EXPECT TO PASS THROUGH THIS WORLD BUT ONCE. ANY GOOD THEREFORE THAT I CAN DO, OR ANY KINDNESS THAT I CAN SHOW TO ANY FELLOW CREATURE, LET ME DO IT NOW. LET ME NOT DEFER OR NEGLECT IT, FOR I SHALL NOT PASS THIS WAY AGAIN.

One of the shocking realities in this world that will take you by surprise when you least expect it is just how quickly your life passes. One day you'll be sitting in math class looking at your watch and wondering when it's going to end and in the blink of an eye you're taking your vitamin supplement to help with that arthritis that's been bothering you lately.

You don't get a second chance at life. Today isn't

25

coming back tomorrow. And the last thing that you want to have happen to you is to be sitting in a rocking chair when you're older and second-guessing the decisions you've made along the road of life. So that plaque hanging in my grandparents' hallway created a sense of urgency for me, especially the part about "I shall not pass this way again."

You'll read in your history books that my era was called the Baby Boomer generation, self-absorbed, and spending lavishly on everything from our homes to our bones. What's really interesting, though, is that there's been a transition from the "Me" to the "We" generation in recent years. The Corporation for National & Community Service reports that baby boomers have a higher rate of volunteerism than seniors or young adults. I believe that the thinking of my generation has evolved to the point of discovering that life isn't all about the almighty ME.

Often times there are dangers in viewing life only from the eyes and not the heart. The eyes have a tendency to be taken prisoner by greed. We see a beautiful new home and we want it. We see a luxurious automobile and we buy it. We see expensive jewelry, brochures for wonderful cruises, and countless other material possessions and we covet them all. For certain, our eyes tell us what we want but it's what's in our heart that defines our genuine needs.

And greed makes us all pay a terrible price, not just financially, but emotionally as well. No better poem explains the fate of those who are obsessed by greed than this one that was sent to me by a friend many years ago.

The Cold Within

(Anonymous)

Six humans trapped by happenstance
In black and bitter cold;
Each one possessed a stick of wood
Or so the story's told.

Their dying fire in need of logs,
The first woman held hers back,
For on the faces around the fire,
She noticed one was black.

The next man sat looking cross the way
Saw one not of his church,
And couldn't bring himself to give
The fire his stick of birch.

The third one sat in tattered clothes.
He gave his coat a hitch.
Why should his log be put to use
To warm the idle rich?

The rich man just sat back and thought
Of the wealth he had in store,
And how to keep what he had earned,
From the lazy, shiftless poor.

The black man's face bespoke revenge

As the fire passed from his sight,
For all he saw in his stick of wood
Was a chance to spite the white.

And the last man of this forlorn group
Did naught except for gain.
Giving only to those who gave,
Was how he played the game.

The logs held tight in death's still hands
Was proof of human sin,
They didn't die from the cold without,
They died from the cold within.

And so, Ethan, I hope you'll always remember that when we die we don't take anything with us. While material possessions can bring us comfort and joy today, none of them can assure us of everlasting happiness tomorrow.

I believe that the satisfaction you will experience in your life will come from those intangible gifts of your heart that you share with others. Don't hold on to your stick of birch. Use your talents, skills, and abilities to keep the fire of life burning.

I love you, Ethan.
Grandpa

> "A life spent making mistakes is
> not only more honorable
> but more useful than a life spent
> in doing nothing."
>
> George Bernard Shaw

DEAR ETHAN:

Of all of the opportunities and challenges that you will face in your life, many of them will involve a certain measure of risk. I took a few risks in my lifetime, some major and some minor. A few of those risks turned out to be mistakes and a few of them produced very positive results.

What I wish that I had been able to learn a bit earlier in my life is that basically there are only three types of risk. And if I had someone explain this information to me a little sooner, maybe my percentage of risk-taking success would have been a little higher. So I'm going to share the three types with you and hope that the information improves your risk success rate.

The first type of risk is the risk that you can afford to take. This is the no-brainer type of risk that one encounters routinely with little worry about the consequences. Giving an opinion in a classroom, asking a girl for a date, or offering to help an elderly person with their groceries can only be met at the very worst with personal rejection. And if that's as bad as life gets, then life isn't too bad. Remember, Jesus was beaten and nailed to a cross.

The second type of risk is the risk that you cannot afford to take. Drinking alcohol and driving, experimenting with drugs, telling malicious lies, and ignoring your personal health and well-being are decisions that could ultimately jeopardize your life. And despite the peer pressure that you might encounter from people who are emotionally weaker than you, whose very existence is centered on the thrill of taking reckless risks, don't let yourself be trapped into a corner from which you may never escape.

Finally, the third type of risk is the most intriguing of all, and that is the risk that you cannot afford not to take. These risks are often times simple, many times subtle and profound.

Pat Tillman was a professional football player who played for the Arizona Cardinals. After the attacks of September 11, 2001, he turned down a three-year, $3.6 million contract from the Cardinals to enlist in the United States Army with his brother. Pat Tillman was killed in a friendly fire incident in Afghanistan while on patrol. Why would an NFL player turn down a lucrative contract to fight a war? For Pat Tillman, I'm sure he perceived it as a risk that he could not afford not to take.

One of the greatest stories ever told about risks is a favorite of mine. It seems that once upon a time there was a powerful king who fell in love with a poor, humble, and lowly maiden in his kingdom. He was so rich and powerful that he believed she would be forever grateful if he married her and made her the queen.

It occurred to him, though, that there would always be something missing in their relationship. She would always admire him, thank him, and respect him; but she would never be able to truly love him because she would always remember her humble origins and her debt of gratitude. The inequality between them would be seemingly insurmountable.

So the king decided that maybe there was another option. He could renounce his kingship, abandon his riches, become a commoner, and then offer the woman his love. In doing this, the king realized that he would be taking a great risk. He would be doing something that would be seen as complete foolishness in the eyes of most people in his kingdom, and perhaps even in her eyes. He would lose his kingship and he may even be rejected by her, especially if she was disappointed at not becoming the queen.

Faced with this choice, the king decided to take the risk. He believed, he said, that "it is better to risk everything to make love possible."

And so, Ethan, risk is an integral part of life. One of the best poems that I've ever read about the reality and implications of risk was given to me by a woman who came to me once for some counseling. I wanted to share this poem with you, and I hope that you'll find it useful in your life's travels.

Risk
(William Arthur Ward)

To laugh is to risk appearing the fool,
To weep is to risk appearing sentimental,
To reach out to another is to risk involvement,
To expose feelings is to risk exposing your true self,
To place your ideas, your dreams before the crowd,
is to risk their loss.
To love is to risk not being loved in return,
To live is to risk dying,
To hope is to risk despair,
To try is to risk failure,
But risk must be taken,
Because the greatest hazard in life is to risk nothing.
The person who risks nothing does nothing, has
nothing, and is nothing.
He may avoid suffering and sorrow,
But he simply cannot learn, feel, change,
grow, love, live.
Chained by his certitudes, he is a slave.
He has forfeited his freedom.
Only a person who risks is free.

I love you, Ethan.
Grandpa

EAR ETHAN:

One of the most challenging times in your life will be
deciding which vocation you decide to pursue. The word
"vocation" will probably sound foreign to you because
today we talk about jobs and careers but seldom vocations.
Understanding the difference among the three will help you
to choose the path where your talents and abilities will best
be used.

I had several jobs when I was a kid. I delivered
newspapers to people's homes during grammar school and
high school, and in college I worked as water-meter reader
to earn money for tuition and spending money. I didn't
like those jobs but I sure liked the money, and even though
I didn't earn all that much, I did feel a certain sense of
satisfaction and accomplishment.

As a marriage and family therapist, I had a career. It

33

was something that I knew that I would do for a long time and I wanted to be the best counselor possible. Physicians, plumbers, teachers, accountants, and electricians are all examples of careers that you learn in school or on the job. You work for a business (or for yourself) and you get paid for employing your talents and skills to help a company or a corporation achieve its business mission.

A vocation, though, is something completely different. Just like its Latin origin, the word vocation implies a "calling," an intangible, most often inexplicable feeling that draws a person to a particular field of endeavor. Passion is the foundation of a vocation and people who respond to that internal calling do so in such a way that nothing is able to deter them from their desired goal.

Some day I want you to ask your Dad about his vocation as a firefighter and EMT. Look at his photo when he was two years old and dressed in his uncle's firefighter helmet and gear. Being a firefighter was his passion growing up and something he never wavered from even when his Mom and I had different ideas about what he might do with his life. Your Dad passionately followed his dream.

It's always been apparent to me that what distinguishes a vocation from a job and a career is that a vocation implies an underlying desire to want to reach out and help others, to touch their lives in a meaningful and positive way.

I've made appointments with doctors who had careers and some who had vocations as true healers. The former were interested in getting me in and out of the office and moving on to the next patient. The latter were interested in me as a person first and then treated my medical concerns. I've met salespeople who were more interested in selling me their product or services than listening to my needs. The former had a job, the latter had a vocation.

Ethan, on your journey to adulthood, I'm sure you'll have some jobs along the way and hopefully you'll enjoy yours more than I did mine when I was growing up. And I know that one day you'll discover a career that blends your talents with your passion, that your developing vocation will be a hope and a help to those that you collaborate with in the years to come.

But what will happen if you pursue what you think is your vocation only to find out several years later that maybe you made a mistake or a bad choice? Not to worry! It happens. Change is a fact of life. Just head back to the drawing board and chart a different course. There's no shame in making a mistake and no shame in altering your life's path.

The important things to remember are to listen to the advice of those who love you and care about you, to weigh your options and opportunities carefully, and to choose a course that will bring you personal and professional happiness.

I love you, Ethan.
Grandpa

DEAR ETHAN:

Some of the most difficult experiences for me in life have
happened when people who were close to me died. In
some instances, death was expected due to health reasons
or age but in others, the death hit me like a hard punch in
the stomach that took my breath away and left me gasping
for air.

When I was younger, I was afraid of death. Growing
up we were taught in religion class that there were
three places you could go when you died—heaven, hell,
or purgatory. If you went to hell you burned in Satan's
flames for having died in mortal sin. That was not a cool
picture. If you went to purgatory you weren't all that bad
but you had to wait awhile and do some penance before
you earned the right to go to heaven. And, of course,
people who died in "the state of grace," or, without sin,
were welcomed immediately into God's kingdom to share
in the joy of everlasting happiness and life.

It's hard to lose someone you love and the subsequent grief brings an emotional pain that can be devastating. Recently, I attended the memorial service for a friend of our family whose nineteen-year-old son committed suicide unexpectedly. He was their only child and manifested no visible signs or warnings that he intended to take his own life. And while he rests comfortably and securely in God's arms today, his parents are left to absorb the pain. No words are adequate consolation. His parents will have to pass through the stages of grief, through the shock, the denial, the anger, and hopefully arrive at a place of reconciliation and hope.

Many years ago I met Sandra, the mother of a seventeen-year-old boy who died in a peaceful night's sleep with no forewarning of any kind. She needed counseling to help manage the intense grief that she was experiencing at the loss of her son. She was particularly appalled at the suggestion of some well-intentioned friends that the arrival of a new grandchild would be a kind of "replacement" for her son.

After several months of therapy, Sandra was able to say good-bye to the son whom she had loved so dearly in this life and hello to the son whose embrace she would feel for all eternity because of her belief in the Incarnation, the Crucifixion, and the Resurrection of Jesus Christ. She made a decision to remember the good times that she had with her Stephen, his many positive attributes as a person, and to carry them in her heart, thereby resurrecting his life within her own until she was reunited with him in heaven.

Ethan, you will lose people that you love in this world.

It's a fact of life. But the most important thing to remember is that your loss is only temporary. The time that we spend in this world is only a flicker of light compared to the everlasting sunshine of eternity.

The promise that God makes to each one of us is that if we use the gifts that He has given to us to build the kingdom of heaven during our journey here on earth, then we will celebrate His presence in our lives as well as all of the lives of our family and friends who have gone before us for all eternity when we die.

When Jesus comforted Martha and Mary on the death of their brother, Lazarus, He said to her, "I am the resurrection and the life; whoever believes in me, even if he dies, will live, and everyone who lives and believes in me will never die. Do you believe this?"

The manner in which each one of us responds to His question to Martha, "Do you believe this?" will determine how we celebrate life and death during our time here on earth. I can tell you that I believe that Jesus is the resurrection and the life and that if we believe in Him, we will live forever.

So when I die, Ethan, I'm going to miss you and hopefully you're going to miss me for just a little while. But always remember the good times that we shared together, keep them in your heart, and when your work is done here on earth, bring them to heaven with you so that we can celebrate for all eternity in God's kingdom.

I love you, Ethan.
Grandpa

EAR ETHAN:

Of the three important gifts that God has given to each one
of us (emotions, intellect, and will) I wanted to share a little
bit with you about each one of them.

From my perspective, the value of our emotions is
vastly underrated. Emotions, not the intellect, connect one
human being to another. While your intellect relies upon
words and thoughts for clarity, emotions can be understood
with a mere glance, a smile, a frown, or a tear.

Emotions can be ecstatically satisfying and rewarding
on the one hand and terribly dangerous on the other. Visiting
a friend in the hospital and sensing their deep appreciation
for the time you spend with them results in positive feelings
that are indescribable. On the other hand, when you're
driving harmlessly down the highway and you're cut off by
a careless driver, the anger you feel could result in behaviors
that are life threatening.

Understanding your emotions and channeling their energies in a positive direction is a challenge that every person faces as they encounter life on a daily basis.

As I studied philosophy, theology, and psychology, I came to understand that there are three fundamental emotional positions that a person can take in life and they are: 1) I will act the way I feel; 2) You will act the way I feel and; 3) I can't help the way I feel right now but I can help the way I think and act.

Emotional position #1, "I will act the way I feel," works pretty well when your emotions are positive. If you feel joyful and you act that way, not much can go wrong. On the other hand, if you feel resentment and you act in a resentful manner, not much can go right. So the first emotional position wouldn't be my favorite.

Emotional position #2, "You will act the way I feel" seems to imply that the world revolves around you and it should sense and react to your personal emotional state. That's just not how the world works despite those who would like it to be that way. If someone says to me "Well, I'm in a great mood and you should be too," I'm not exactly convinced that a lot of empathy is flowing my way.

So what has worked for me best over the years is emotional position #3, "I can't help the way I feel right now, but I can help the way I think and act."

Emotions are neither right nor wrong, Ethan. They can come upon us in an instant and disappear just as quickly. People who navigate life and relationships successfully find a way to balance their emotions with their intellect and will, choosing the best course of action in a given situation.

A young man came to see me many years ago for some advice. Ron was about thirty-five years old and had worked for the same family-owned manufacturing company since he graduated from high school. He was a motivated self-starter who was able to maintain his full-time job and earn a college degree at the same time.

Despite his long-term success and longevity at work, he was recently passed over for a major promotion, which left him angry and depressed. He talked about quitting, starting a new career, and moving to a different part of the country for a fresh start.

Using that third emotional position, he couldn't help the way he felt when he experienced his disappointment. Fortunately, he could control his thoughts and actions, and decided that marching into the CEO's office to give him a piece of his mind wasn't exactly the smartest thing to do in the long run. He stayed the course, put his nose back to the grindstone, and worked harder than he had before to help the company accomplish its business goals.

Five years later when the owner of the company died, Ron was unexpectedly invited to the reading of the will. What Ron never knew was that he had always been admired and respected by upper management and, in particular, the owner. They especially admired the way he handled the disappointment of not being made a vice president and the maturity and dedication that he had evidenced the past five years.

In his will, the owner named him as COO (Chief

Operating Officer) of the business as well as a primary stockholder of the company.

While learning to manage your emotions doesn't always produce such extraordinary results, Ron's story gives testimony to the benefit of balancing your emotions, intellect, and will for the purpose accomplishing your personal and business goals.

As you go through life, Ethan, and experience all of the challenges and opportunities that it has to offer, remember to use your emotions to empathize and connect with others in a positive way. Don't let negative, impulsive, emotional reactions negate the investment that you have in your relationships with family, friends, and co-workers.

I love you, Ethan.
Grandpa

DEAR ETHAN:

Of the intellect, emotions, and will, the intellect is that power of our mind which allows us to know and understand the world around us. And as we grow in our knowledge and understanding of the world, we have the ability to make a positive difference in the lives of those around us. Unfortunately, the converse is also true. There are people who choose, for whatever reason, to make knowledge a weapon and use it to harm others.

When I was growing up I wasn't the smartest kid in my class. In high school, there were five freshman classes with the real bright kids in the 9-1 division, which represented the ninth year, number one class all the way down to 9-5, which represented the lowest class. I was in 9-3, so I got the impression that I was just about average.

In all of my education right through college, I learned a lot about a variety of topics. Philosophy, theology, and psychology were the fields that really intrigued me so I devoted my energies to learning more about human behavior and our spiritual nature.

As you grow up and begin your academic pursuits, you'll take all of the fundamental courses in school. Eventually, you'll find some areas that interest you more than others and your attention will be focused there as you discover and build your vocation in life.

When I think about you growing up and going to school, I remember a quote from the Spanish painter and sculptor Pablo Picasso. He said, "It takes a long time to become young." I remember in your first year of life how curious you were about everything, everywhere, and everyone. Your hands and your eyes would explore the world around you intently. Whether you heard the garage door open, a siren in the distance, a plane flying overhead, or a dog barking down the street, your attention became instantly devoted to the source of the sound. When I would walk with you through the mall at Christmas you were enchanted by the decorations, the lights, and the texture of the ornaments on the wreaths hanging in the stores. You stopped to study the faces of the people in the food court, and we rode up and down the escalators continually because the dynamics of the ride enthralled you.

If you carry that curiosity and wonder of life with you throughout your school years, your experiences will be very rewarding and fulfilling. Unfortunately, as we grow older, we drift away from the learning styles that shaped our early childhood, and the classroom becomes a collection of tests, quizzes, and pressures that defeat the very purpose of learning.

While I wouldn't want you to repeat this course of action, the strategy of the Pulitzer Prize-winning author Upton Sinclair speaks loudly to the thirst for genuine learning. When Sinclair wanted to attend college he couldn't raise the required amount necessary to pay for his tuition.

However, as he perused the college catalogue, he discovered that if a student failed a course, although he received no credit for that course, he was, nevertheless, required to take another course in its place. There was no charge for the additional class because he had already paid once for his credit.

Realizing the dubious opportunity at hand, Sinclair took advantage of the policy and received a free college education by deliberately failing all of his classes. Upton Sinclair confided that "earning a degree" was not as important to him as "acquiring the knowledge" he needed to pursue his dream.

What's most important to remember, Ethan, is that the power of your intellect is not restricted to what you learn in school. There is a wealth of knowledge available in books, places, and people.

Life itself is a learning experience and you'll soon discover that no one has a monopoly on "right ideas" or the "best ways" to accomplish things. In addition, just because people graduate from high school or college or earn some advanced degree, that doesn't mean that learning stops. If you interviewed the most educated people in the world, the honest ones would tell you that learning is a journey that never ends.

Your lifelong learning process began when you were born and will continue until the day you die. Hopefully, you'll have great teachers and mentors along the way who will stimulate your mind and engage your imagination so that your tremendous gifts will be a blessing to those whose lives you touch.

I love you, Ethan.
Grandpa

"The will to win, the desire to succeed, the urge
to reach your full potential ... these are the keys
that will unlock the door to personal excellence."

Confucius

EAR ETHAN:

Since we've already talked about two of the three great gifts
that God has given to you, your emotions and your intellect,
now is the time for me to share with you some thoughts on
the third and perhaps most important gift, your will.

Life is certainly full of extremely intelligent people with
a solid emotional framework who seldom, if ever, meet with
success in any aspect of life and people wonder, *Why?* The
answer is simple, but sad. They never employed their will;
they never demonstrated the drive that it takes to achieve
their goals.

On the other hand, the world is also full of people of
average intelligence who achieve extraordinary results
in their chosen field and observers seem incredulous that
such great results could be produced by ordinary, everyday
individuals and they ask, "How did they do that?"

Once again, the answer is simple, but not so obvious.
They reached deep down into their guts and summoned the

power of their wills to reach beyond what is merely possible to attain what they may have thought to be impossible.

A few months before your Dad was born, I stayed up late to watch the Olympic ice hockey game between the United States and the Soviet Union at Lake Placid, New York. As it turned out, it was arguably the most incredible display of will and desire that I've ever seen in an athletic competition in my lifetime.

The odds against a win by the United States were astronomical. The day before the game, columnist Dave Anderson wrote in the *New York Times*, "Unless the ice melts, or unless the United States team or another team performs a miracle, as did the American squad in 1960, the Russians are expected to easily win the gold medal for the sixth time in the last seven tournaments." The problem was that somebody forgot to tell the American college kids that they were supposed to lose.

In exhibition games during the Olympic year, the Russians went 5-3-1 against teams from the National Hockey League (NHL), and in the prior year they embarrassed the NHL All-Stars 6-0 to win the Challenge Cup. Their goaltender, Vladislav Tretiak, was viewed by many as the number one goaltender in the world at that time. In addition, the Soviet players, classified as amateurs, essentially played professionally in an established league in the Soviet Union and many of their players were active-duty soldiers in the Red Army. And less than two weeks earlier, the United States met those same Russians in an exhibition game in Madison Square Garden in New York and were soundly beaten, 10-3.

Today, Ethan, and most likely for all time, that hockey game will always be referred to as the "miracle on ice." The U.S. fell behind early 1-0, then 2-1, and 3-2 before taking a 4-3 lead with exactly ten minutes remaining. It was a classic David versus Goliath confrontation and you could see the looks in the eyes of the young American players that they would not be denied after they had clawed their way to the lead.

As time wound down in the game and pandemonium prevailed in the stands, ABC sportscaster Al Michaels, who called the game with Montreal Canadiens goalie Ken Dryden, broadcast the final seconds in words that are forever etched in our memories: "Eleven seconds, you've got ten seconds, the countdown going on right now! Morrow, up to Silk. Five seconds left in the game. Do you believe in miracles? YES!"

Sports Illustrated, in its March 3, 1980, issue did something that it had never done in its history. It showed a photograph by Heinz Klutmeier capturing the game's conclusion with no accompanying caption or headline. Klutmeier said, "It didn't need it. Everyone in America knew what happened." The stunning victory was voted as the greatest sports moment in the twentieth century by *Sports Illustrated*. And, by the way, that was not even the gold medal game. The U.S. still had to come back and beat Finland 2-1 to actually win Olympic gold.

What that experience demonstrated to me is that against all odds, the power of an individual's will and desire can overcome any apparently insurmountable obstacle. In addition, when a group of people from different backgrounds and philosophies come together and put aside their differences to accomplish a single goal, the results can be nothing short of phenomenal.

So always remember, Ethan, that while your intellect and emotions are two very important gifts, it's your will that makes things happen and produces the results that you hope to achieve.

If you have a thought or an idea, share it. If you feel something, express it constructively. Most of all, empower yourself to be the master of your own fate; chart your course in life, follow it, and don't let anyone or anything stand in your way.

I love you, Ethan.
Grandpa

"Integrity has no need of rules."

—— Albert Camus

*D*EAR ETHAN:

One of the greatest qualities that any human being can possess is integrity. It's not something that you inherit from your parents or learn from your teachers; although both your parents and your teachers can help you shape your identity of integrity.

In the dictionaries and textbooks, integrity means adhering to a code of ethics, keeping your word, and being honest in all of your relationships with others. Integrity implies sincerity, fairness, justice, and doing the right thing.

In real life, integrity is a priceless commodity that takes years to nurture and strengthen and only a split second to destroy. The poet Ralph Waldo Emerson underscored the value of integrity when he wrote, "Nothing is at last sacred but the integrity of your own mind."

When I was a child I remember being told the story about an Emperor living in the Far East who knew that his health was beginning to fail and that it was time to prepare a successor for his kingdom. He decided, though, that he would not follow the customary succession plan of appointing one of his assistants or even a member of his own family. Instead, he decided that he would prepare one of the children in his kingdom to assume the duties of Emperor when he could no longer discharge his responsibilities.

So one day he called all of the children together and told them of his plan. He said, "I am going to give each one of you a seed, just one seed. And it is a very special seed. I want you to take it home, plant it, water it, grow it, and in exactly one year I want you to bring me back the results of your work. I will then judge the plants that you bring to me and I will select the new Emperor at that time."

So all of the children returned to their homes with great excitement and did as the Emperor requested. There was a young boy in the group whose name was Ling and he anxiously rushed to his house and told the story to his mother. They both went out and purchased a pot in which to plant the seed and when they arrived back home they began the process with great care.

About three weeks later some of Ling's classmates came to school and started talking about their plants and how they were beginning to show signs of growth, so Ling ran home at the end of the day but found nothing. After one month, two months, and throughout the balance of the year, while the other children would boast about their amazing plants, Ling would only become more discouraged and depressed because in his pot there was no sign of life.

The day had finally come for all of the children to return to the Emperor with the plants. Ling, embarrassed and ashamed, didn't want to go and even became sick to his stomach. His mother, though, encouraged him to go, to be honest about what had happened and face the Emperor. Ling knew she was right so he took his pot and went to meet the other children and the Emperor.

When he arrived, he was amazed at the variety of beautiful plants that his peers had grown with their seed throughout the year. Ling, however, just found a place to stand in the back of the room and placed his pot on the floor. Many of the other kids just laughed at him when they saw his results and others just said, "Nice try!"

When the Emperor came to the gathering, he, too, marveled at all of the beautiful plants and remarked, "One of you will be the next Emperor of our kingdom."

As the Emperor walked around the stage he noticed Ling standing in the back of the room with his empty pot. He ordered his guards to bring Ling forward. Ling was terrified, thinking that he failed so terribly that he would either be expelled from the kingdom or killed.

As the children were laughing at him and making fun of him, the Emperor ordered the crowd to be silent. Then he said, "Behold your new Emperor. His name is Ling." There was a gasp of astonishment and a hush fell over the crowd. Ling couldn't believe it. He couldn't even grow the seed. How could he be named as the new Emperor?

The Emperor spoke, "One year ago today I gave each one of you a single seed to grow. But I gave you all boiled seeds which would not grow. All of you except Ling brought me back beautiful plants and flowers. When the first seed did not grow, you went out and substituted another seed in its place. Ling was the only one who had the courage and the integrity to bring me the pot with my seed in it. Therefore, he will be the new Emperor."

Ethan, to the extent that you are a person of integrity as you grow up and live your life, success will find you in your personal and business relationships. However, as I mentioned to you earlier, it only takes a split second to destroy integrity with a lie, a dishonest transaction, or a trust betrayed.

So if you're wondering how you're progressing along the road of integrity, here's a poem that your great-grandfather gave to me many years ago. Hopefully, it will guide you along the way.

The Man in the Glass
(Adapted from a poem by Peter "Dale" Wimbrow Sr.)

When you get what you want in your struggle for self
And the world makes you king for a day,
Just go to the mirror and look at yourself
And see what that man has to say.

For it isn't your father or mother or wife
Whose judgment upon you must pass.
The fellow whose verdict counts most in your life
Is the one staring back from the glass.

You may be like Jack Horner and chisel a plum
And think you're a wonderful guy.
But the man in the glass says you're only a bum
If you can't look him straight in the eye.

He's the fellow to please—never mind all the rest,
For he's with you clear to the end.
And you've passed your most dangerous, difficult test
If the man in the glass is your friend.

You may fool the whole world down the pathway of years
And get pats on the back as you pass.
But your final reward will be heartache and tears
If you've cheated the man in the glass.

I love you, Ethan.
Grandpa

———— ❧ ————

"When we honestly ask ourselves which
person in our lives means the most to us,
we often find that it is those who, instead
of giving advice, solutions, or cures, have
chosen rather to share our pain and touch our
wounds with a warm and tender hand."

———— ❧ ————

Henri Nouwen

DEAR ETHAN:

I want to share with you some of my thoughts on one of the most fascinating and rewarding experiences in life and that is friendship.

In your life you'll have friends that you play with as a child, friends in school, and friends throughout your teenage years and your adult life. Many of your friends will be good ones and fun to be around while others will disappoint you, hurt you, and betray your trust.

What I learned about friendship as I grew into adulthood is that there's a pretty significant difference between an acquaintance and a friend. While I might enjoy going to a baseball game with an acquaintance, I wouldn't necessarily look to that person for the emotional support that I'd expect

59

from a friend.

Now, in my later years, looking back on my life, I can honestly say that while I had many positive, mutually beneficial and helpful acquaintances throughout the years, the number of true friendships that I experienced were few. It takes time, patience, commitment, and empathy to be a true friend.

Mary Anne Evans (who wrote under the pen name of George Eliot) offered a thought about friendship that rang true with me: "Friendship is the inexpressible comfort of feeling safe with a person, having neither to weigh thoughts nor measure words." When you have a true friend, you will always feel that person's compassion and the trust that fortifies your bond.

The impact of experiencing a genuine friendship was described so powerfully in a story that I had read several years ago on the Internet. It became known as "The Friendship Story," and while events like the one described here aren't commonplace, they do happen, and we just never know how our words and actions can affect the fate of a complete stranger.

The Friendship Story

One day when I was a freshman in high school, I saw the new kid in my class walking home from school. His name was Kyle. It looked like he was carrying all of his books. I thought to myself, *Why would anyone bring home all his books on Friday? He must really be a nerd.* I had quite a weekend planned with parties and a football game. So I shrugged my shoulders and walked on.

Just then a bunch of kids ran towards him, knocking the books out of his arms and tripping him so he landed in the dirt. His glasses went flying, and I saw them land in the grass about ten feet from him. As he looked up, I saw a terrible sadness in his eyes. My heart went out to him. I jogged over to him, picked up the glasses and handed them to him.

"Those guys are jerks. They should really get lives," I commented.

He looked at me and said, "Hey, thanks!" There was a big smile on his face. It was one of those smiles that showed real gratitude.

I helped him pick up his books and asked him where he lived. As it turned out, he lived near me. As we walked home, I discovered he was a pretty cool kid. I asked him if he would like to play football with me and my friends on Saturday. He said, "Yes." We hung out together all weekend and the more I got to know Kyle, the more I liked him. My friends liked him too.

On Monday morning, I saw Kyle carrying his huge stack of books again. I stopped him and said, "Dang, boy, you are gonna really build some serious muscle

carrying this pile of books everyday!"
He laughed and handed me half the books.

Over the next four years, Kyle and I became best
friends. By our senior year, Kyle had filled out and
looked great. He was one of those guys that really
found himself during high school. All the girls loved
him, and he always had lots of dates. He had studied
hard and was valedictorian of our class.

On graduation day, he was to give a speech. I could see
that he was nervous. So I smacked him on the back and
said, "Hey, big guy, you'll be great!" He looked at me
with one of those grateful looks and smiled, "Thanks."

He started his speech by saying, "Graduation is a time
to thank those who helped you make it through those
tough years: your parents, your teachers, your siblings,
maybe a coach, but mostly your friends. I am here to
tell you that being a friend to someone is the best gift
you can give."

Then he began to tell the story of the first day we met.
I stared at him in disbelief when he told how he had
planned to kill himself that weekend. He had cleaned
out his locker so his mom wouldn't have to do it later.
I heard a gasp go through the crowd as this handsome
and popular boy told about his weakest moment.

He looked hard at me, gave me a little smile, and said, "Thankfully, my friend saved me from doing the unspeakable."

His mom and dad looked at me with a grateful nod. Not until that moment did I realize that in one small gesture I changed a person's life. Now I never underestimate the power of my actions. I learned that the support of a caring friend can impact someone in ways we may not fully understand and appreciate.

So, Ethan, I hope that you are blessed in your life with true friendships that bring you much happiness, laughter, joy, and satisfaction. The value of such a relationship was best described in the Old Testament book of Sirach: "A faithful friend is a sturdy shelter; he who finds one finds a treasure. A faithful friend is beyond price, no sum can balance his worth."

I love you, Ethan.
Grandpa

"Whenever you're in conflict with someone,
there is one factor that can make the difference
between damaging your relationship and
deepening it. That factor is attitude."

———— William James

*D*EAR ETHAN:

In the course of human relationships, conflict is inevitable.
Husbands and wives find themselves mired in arguments;
athletes get upset with their coaches, and friends fight over
lovers and loyalty.

The ultimate outcome of conflict can either be
catastrophic in that it ends in additional stress and fractured
relationships, or it can be constructive in that there is a new
peace and harmony as well as hope for a stronger bond. It
all depends upon the method used to resolve the conflict
and there are essentially five choices for conflict resolution.
Each of the five choices can be appropriate or inappropriate
to employ depending upon the situation.

First, there is the power response to conflict. "Do it
because I said so," is language that usually describes this
method for handling conflict. If the issue is important in

an adult-to-adult conversation, this means to a resolution is highly ineffective and can result in the breakdown of all communication between the two parties.

On the other hand, if you're the parent driving down the highway and your two kids in the back seat are needlessly arguing about what restaurant gets your business for dinner, you can simply end the discussion by selecting a place yourself. And while there may be temporary moans and groans, the issue is quickly forgotten on a full stomach.

Secondly, you can deny that any conflict exists. Choosing that response to a genuine conflict may be a temporary band-aid but it is totally useless if the contested issue is important to at least one of the parties. However, if the issue is trivial, like arguing with my brother about the quality of professional hockey in Florida, there's no reason to continue to acknowledge that type of absurdity. (By the way, Bob, when was the last time the Rangers won a Stanley Cup?)

The third recourse for managing conflict is suppression. A cousin of denial, suppression realizes the presence of the conflict but, rather than facing it head-on, just hopes that it will go away soon. When the issue is important, suppression doesn't work because the gravity of the conflict only escalates in intensity the longer it is ignored.

For example, the disgruntled yet gifted athlete whose behavior creates ongoing problems for the franchise is not disciplined by ownership in the hopes that someday his behavior will improve. The gamble doesn't pay off, things get worse, and team morale sinks to a new low. Suppression was not the answer.

On the other hand, suppression is a useful tool when the conflict is frivolous to both parties and the time dedicated to resolving it would not be a wise investment.

Compromise is the fourth tool for managing conflict. When the issue is important, both parties say, "I'm willing to give a little here" to reach a solution. The end result is not the perfect outcome that they had in mind, but it's a resolution that satisfies both parties, thereby enabling them to move forward in the relationship or put an end to the issue that precipitated the conflict.

Compromise is a great choice when both parties have the time to devote to achieving a compromise. However, when the conflict is urgent and the matter grave, perhaps the power response is a more appropriate choice.

The fifth and final option for resolving a conflict is collaboration. Simply, when this method is used to overcome conflict both parties set aside their preconceived notions about what needs to be done. Instead, with a spirit of cooperation, they proceed to craft a single solution that they can claim as their own. With collaboration, there is no hidden agenda, no bargaining, no selfishness, and no hesitation to genuinely working together for a good that benefits both parties.

When time is available to invest in a constructive solution, collaboration is the first choice for conflict resolution as it achieves the greatest commitment to long-term success.

Ethan, in the course of your life you'll be involved in

more than your share of conflicts, some bigger than others. The way that you choose to manage those conflicts will determine whether stress or success is your more frequent companion. Hopefully, your assessment of the nature of the conflict will enable you to employ a resolution strategy that eliminates potentially challenging obstacles in both your personal and professional life.

And remember, conflicts are a normal and natural occurrence along the road of life. Don't let them cause you any undue grief or anxiety as you pursue your dreams.

I love you, Ethan.
Grandpa

"The greatest wealth is health."

Virgil

*D*EAR ETHAN:

Our health is a precious gift. From the day we're born into this imperfect world, our internal body clock is ticking until the day that we are called to our heavenly home. And because our lives are one of the many gifts that God has given to us, it becomes our responsibility to care for our bodies, as well as our minds and our souls.

Your great-grandfather, Joe McQueen, died when he was fifty-nine years old of cardiovascular disease. He had a sedentary job, smoked, ate the wrong foods, battled his weight, and only had time to play golf once a week for exercise. Of course, in those days, people didn't have the benefit of what medical science has discovered recently about what constitutes a healthy lifestyle.

Hopefully, in your adult years, you and your loved ones will benefit from ongoing research that is designed to win the war against heart disease, cancer, Alzheimer's disease, and other sicknesses that cause premature suffering and death today.

When your Dad was born, I made a commitment to exorcise my own weight demons with a solid fitness plan that I maintain even today. I started jogging regularly, worked with a fitness instructor, and made it to the gym as often as possible. Having a son and being responsible for his growth and development was not a responsibility that I took lightly. Selfishly, I wanted to enjoy as much time with your Dad in this world as I possibly could. Of course, now that you're here, Ethan, I have a renewed energy and purpose for staying healthy and enjoying every single minute that I can with you.

And after a lifetime of listening to all sorts of advice about what a person needs to do to establish good health, I've condensed all of it into a few basic tips that I want to share with you:

✔ Healthy living is a lifelong process. Being healthy shouldn't be a New Year's resolution that you work on for a few weeks every January and then forget about for the rest of the year. Make your physical and emotional health a priority so that you can enjoy your friends and family well into your senior years.

✔ Be knowledgeable about vitamins, supplements, and natural remedies that promote good health. In addition, not all vitamins and supplements are created equal. Find companies that produce reputable products. Unfortunately, the vitamin supplement industry today has its share of charlatans that produce inferior and sometimes dangerous, life-threatening products that do more harm than good.

✔ Don't assume that just because you're healthy you don't need to see a doctor. Find a physician that you can trust and get regular checkups. Preventative medicine is largely underrated. Do your due diligence and ensure that the medical professionals you consult with are credible, competent, compassionate, and that they don't foster dependency.

✔ A well-designed exercise program is a worthwhile investment of time and money. The combination of a cardiovascular workout and weight training five days a week on a regular basis can alleviate the onset of many age-related health concerns in addition to replenishing your physical energy and enhancing your emotional energy as you face life's daily trials and tribulations.

✔ The best medical advice that I ever received was to never go on a diet. After a wonderful physician/ nutritionist empowered me with that thought, I lost thirty pounds by just eating smaller meal portions more frequently—not exactly rocket science. I wish I had learned sooner that diets are not only a ridiculous waste of time but they can actually make it harder for you to lose weight as you advance in years.

So Ethan, to the extent that you care for your body and maintain a healthy lifestyle, you'll be increasing your chances for living a long and happy life while nurturing and respecting the gifts of body, mind, and soul that God has given to you.

I love you, Ethan.
Grandpa

DEAR ETHAN:

To talk about love and the significance that it has in our lives is one of the most difficult challenges that any human being can face. Love can be the supreme ecstasy of a joy-filled life or the ultimate tragedy of a bitter and lonely existence. Ultimately, love is a choice for which we celebrate what has been found, or mourn what must be lost.

During my years as a marriage and family therapist, I saw thousands of couples in individual and group settings who were seeking help for their relationships. Most of them were very nice people who never had a solid foundation in the nature of genuine love.

In terms of a marriage relationship, there are three cyclical phases of love:

1. The first phase is romantic love. This phase involves romance, sensuality, and sexuality. It's where we hear most often the phrase "falling in love," as the

initial attraction of the couple is heavily hormonal and emotional. Unfortunately many naive couples base their decision to marry on the fulfillment that they experience in this phase. The overwhelming majority of couples who marry without experiencing the two remaining phases of marital love eventually separate or divorce.

2. The second phase is projective love. As time passes and the couple acquires a more in-depth knowledge of their partner, they begin to project their needs onto that person and attempt to determine if those needs will be met in the long-term. For example, "Will my husband really be able to listen to me when I need someone to talk to?" Or, he will wonder, "Does my wife have the patience to understand the demands of my career?" The majority of marriages today fall in those first two phases of love. That's why the current divorce rate in American is about 50 percent.

3. The third phase is conscious love. Fundamentally, conscious love is based upon the attitude of both the husband and the wife that, without compromising their ethics, morals, and integrity, they will do whatever it takes to make the relationship work. Communication fuels conscious love. Summarizing the importance of positive and productive dialogue, one insightful spouse told me once that "communication is to marriage what blood is to the

body; if it's not flowing all of the time, you have a relationship but no life."

Hopefully, Ethan, the institution of marriage will become stronger than it is today as you grow up. When about half of a country's marriages end because of divorce, it's obvious that the conscious love component that is required to survive and thrive in marriage is sorely absent.

Marriage is a serious commitment, not a convenience. And when relationships don't work and couples fail to establish a solid foundation for their future, it's been my experience as a therapist that there are five formidable roadblocks that derail their progress:

1. Fear of Intimacy: This roadblock suggests that if your spouse gets too close to you, somehow, too much of your real personality will be discovered. Because this knowledge makes you vulnerable, you attempt to maintain an emotional distance from your spouse.

2. Need for Power: This roadblock occurs when you feel that you must control or exert the most power in a relationship. To do anything less implies that you are ineffective in your married life.

3. Low Self-Esteem: This roadblock suggests that you are worthless, of no value, and can contribute nothing positive in your relationship with your spouse. Since you have nothing to offer, you take

no initiative with your partner and most likely feel inferior, defensive, or tentative.

4. Mistrust: This roadblock causes you to doubt that your spouse really likes and accepts who you are rather than how he or she wants you to be. Therefore, you keep your guard up to avoid being taken advantage of in the relationship.

5. Idealized Marital Image: This roadblock suggests that you know how a relationship "should be" and what actions need to happen to get you to that point. Usually, the standards are so idealistic and unrealistic that they are rendered unobtainable. You stop trying and that results in depression and a lack of marital satisfaction.

Ethan, if and when you decide to get married, I hope that you'll remember the phases of love and the basic roadblocks to a healthy relationship. But, more importantly, I pray that you will always remember how important it is to build your relationship with your spouse on the personal relationship each of you have with God and the love He has for the both of you.

Keep in mind the importance of communication in marriage and know that prayer is the pinnacle of all communication. Praying together as a couple and as a family goes a long way toward experiencing the support and the blessings that God has for His children.

Finally, there's been an abundance of material written on the meaning of love and marriage. But nothing describes the essence of love required to make a marriage work better than the words written by St. Paul in his letter to the Corinthians, a passage that is read often at weddings but heeded in the long-term all too infrequently. Ethan, I hope you take these words to heart, and if you do, you will enjoy a life of love that is richly blessed:

> Set your heart on the greater gifts. I will show you the way which surpasses all others. If I speak with human tongues and angelic as well, but do not have love, I am a noisy gong, a clanging symbol. If I have the gift of prophecy and, with full knowledge, comprehend all mysteries, if I have faith great enough to move mountains, but have not love, I am nothing. If I give everything I have to feed the poor and hand over my body to be burned, but have not love, I gain nothing. Love is patient; love is kind. Love is not jealous, it does not put on airs, it is not snobbish. Love is never rude, it is not self-seeking, it is not prone to anger; neither does it brood over injuries. Love does not rejoice in what is wrong but rejoices with the truth. There is no limit to love's forbearance, to its trust, its hope, its power to endure. Love never fails.

And my love for you, Ethan, will never fail.
Grandpa

> "Children are not casual guests in our
> home. They have been loaned to us
> temporarily for the purpose of loving them
> and instilling a foundation of values on
> which their future lives will be built."
>
> Dr. James Dobson

 EAR ETHAN:

When you grow up you may have children of your own. Maybe you'll coach your son or daughter in soccer or baseball. Or you might find yourself in a classroom teaching young minds. There's no question that in your life you're going to have many opportunities to influence the lives of children. It's an awesome responsibility and a priceless gift. The character of a society is defined by its commitment to its youth.

Unfortunately, in my generation, we haven't done the best job possible caring for our kids. Child abuse, poverty, addiction, suicide, obesity, and divorce are just a few of the major obstacles that impede the healthy development of children today. In addition, parents who are ill-equipped to raise their children foster unhealthy environments that result in long-term physical and emotional consequences.

I remember coaching your Dad in T-ball and then baseball right through high school. The Little League years were the most interesting. There was one game in particular that's etched in my mind, although, sad to say, that experience is by no means an isolated one. It happened in a pretty close contest when one of my ten-year-olds came up to bat at a very critical time.

His father was standing behind the backstop as he was accustomed to do. On this day, however, he was particularly obnoxious. His son, Jay, had just struck out swinging when Dad decided to yell at him and berate him on his way back to the dugout. "Only an idiot swings at pitches like those," he shouted. "I don't know why I spend any time with you trying to teach you anything. Nothing sinks into that thick skull of yours," he yelled, and he just wouldn't stop harassing his son.

When Jay got back to the dugout, he wasn't crying but I saw the tears in his eyes. It broke my heart that a good kid had to endure that kind of humiliation from his father in front of his peers and plenty of spectators in the stands.

What was even more discouraging was that after the game when I had an opportunity to meet with Jay's dad, he still didn't get it. He denied any wrongdoing and promptly told me in no uncertain terms that he'd talk to his own child in any way he saw fit.

Having witnessed too many kids being crushed by the senseless behavior of adults over the years, I developed what I call "The Ten Demandments" for parents and other adults who are charged with the responsibility of creating a healthy and nurturing environment for children. I hope that you'll find them meaningful in your adult life.

The Ten Demandments

1. Give kids some room to grow. Create and maintain a friendly and cooperative living environment while respecting their individuality and freedom.

2. Love your children enough to make them want to adhere to your reasonable expectations.

3. Maintain the highest respect for your children's feelings and empathize with those feelings without fail.

4. When you discipline your children, make certain that the consequences are related to the offense, or the lesson will be lost.

5. Invest time in your children. When you tell them, "I don't have time," then you might as well add "… for you."

6. Always acknowledge and commend good behavior. Do whatever you can to encourage independence and competence.

7. Allow your children to experience the freedom of imperfection. Teach them that mistakes are the building blocks of life.

8. Understand that your children experience stress and make allowances for them during stressful times.

9. Model behavior for your children that reflects the highest values and morals. Be consistent and avoid double standards.

10. Share with them a faith in God. Pray together and help them to understand what it means to be "created in the image and likeness of God."

Being a good role model for children isn't rocket science—it's common sense. And when you condense all of the books and articles that have ever been written on facilitating the development of a child that is physically, emotionally, intellectually, socially, and spiritually well-adjusted, nothing sums up the advice better than this story.

In his book, *Man's Search for Meaning,* psychiatrist and Holocaust survivor Viktor Frankl wrote that while the will of many prisoners crumbled in the terror of the Nazi death camps in World War II, a good number were able to survive. Being a psychotherapist and a prisoner himself, he couldn't help but ask the question, "How?" What gave them the ability to endure the torture, the isolation, and the hopelessness?

He came to the conclusion that the survivors of those death camps were people who deeply believed that their lives had meaning. Dr. Frankl further observed that a prisoner's faith gave meaning to his existence. That faith generated an energy that uplifted one's humanity.

Dr. Frankl discerned the significance of his own existence when he wrote:

> A thought transfixed me: For the first time in my life, I saw the truth as it is set into song by so many poets, proclaimed as the final wisdom by so many thinkers. The truth—that love is the ultimate and highest goal to which man can aspire. Then I grasped the meaning of the greatest secret that human poetry and human thought have to impart: the salvation of man is through love and in love.

So what I want to share with you, Ethan, is that I believe the greatest thing we can do for our children and those entrusted to our care throughout the years, is to communicate to them by our words and actions that God loves them, that we love them, and that their lives have meaning. When children know, feel, and experience those three truths, they grow up with a strong sense of personal fulfillment as well as a solid foundation that will enable them to discover and develop their unique talents and abilities for the benefit of all humanity.

And, finally, I want you to know, Ethan, that God truly does love you. I love you. And your life has a very special meaning and purpose.

I love you, Ethan.
Grandpa

EAR ETHAN:

When Wayne Gretzky is revered as "The Great One" by his
countless fans throughout the world, it's not just a nickname.
He truly is the most legendary hockey player to have ever
laced up a pair of skates. When #99 retired in 1999, he held
or shared at least sixty-one records in the National Hockey
League. Among his incredible list of accomplishments, he
was named as *Sports Illustrated*'s "Hockey Player of the
Century."

And while Wayne Gretzky scored a lot of goals in his
career as a player, don't think for one minute that he didn't
have a lot of personal and professional goals as well. No
athlete having attained his level of accomplishment wakes
up every day without a plan for self-improvement.

Goals are incredibly helpful in moving people and
businesses in the direction of the end results that they want
to achieve. Unfortunately, goals can also be incredibly
dangerous when they focus too much attention on the
ultimate "end" result rather than the "means" to reach a

particular outcome. For example, it's a great goal to want to be licensed as a registered nurse. That goal becomes problematic when fulfilling licensing requirements and continuing education assignments becomes more important than the actual ministry of nursing and touching patient's lives.

The number of goals that a person has is of zero importance. What really matters is the quality of those goals as they relate to the development and employment of the individual's unique gifts and talents. Goals can be personal, professional, spiritual, emotional, physical, and financial among others. The key is to establish goals that make sense. And sensible goals have four clearly defined attributes: they are specific, measurable, achievable, and time-related.

I used to say, Ethan, that my goal was to lose some weight. I didn't for the longest time. My goal wasn't specific, measureable, achievable, or time-related. Eventually, I became goal-smart and said, "I want to lose twenty pounds in three months." I did accomplish that goal and focused on the means to get there, like eating responsibly and exercising efficiently.

Meaningful goals keep our lives on track and moving in a positive direction. I read a study once from the Harvard Business School on what made the difference between success and failure in the lives of people with similar backgrounds and educational styles.

The study shocked me because it concluded that 3 percent of people were successful, 30 percent were moderately successful, and that 67 percent just exist. The researchers said that the 3 percent had very specific goals written down, the 30 percent had a general idea about what they wanted to do but no concrete goals, and the 67 percent were content with no real direction in life.

What was really interesting is that the study also concluded that the people in the 30 percent group needed only to put a small amount of effort into formalizing their plans with clear, specific goals and strategies to move into the higher success category.

People don't set goals for a number of reasons: they don't know how, they're too busy, they have a fear of failure, they have a fear of success, or they're preoccupied being what others want them to be rather than defining their own purpose and mission in life. Whatever the reason, the bottom line is that the greatest stress in life comes from feeling powerless and out of control. And having no goals not only puts us into that "just exist" category, but a goal-less life can lead to stresses and anxieties that we don't need to bear.

As you grow older, Ethan, the benefits of goal-setting will be more evident to you. Goals will give your life a clear sense of purpose and direction; they generate enthusiasm for what you want to accomplish and guide you in your journey toward ultimate success. In addition, goals enrich your sense of self-esteem as you accomplish them, maximize your use of time, and make life a more enjoyable as well as a productive journey.

I didn't realize it at the time, but my goal-setting efforts began many years ago with a single piece of paper on which

I wrote at the top "TO DO." There may have been five to ten items on the list at any given time. As I crossed out each one after having accomplished the task, I felt a small sense of pride and satisfaction. That "TO DO" list later blossomed into a purpose and goal-setting plan characterized by the four qualities I mentioned earlier.

For the time that you invest in establishing meaningful goals in your life, the payoff is more than worth the effort.

And today, Ethan, one of my most important goals is to be the best grandfather that I can be everyday by loving you, being present in your life, and sharing my life's experiences with you for the purpose of enriching yours.

I love you, Ethan.
Grandpa

"A thankful heart is not only the greatest
virtue, but the parent of all the other virtues."

Cicero

$\mathcal{D}$EAR ETHAN:

One of my favorite days of the year has always been
Thanksgiving. I remember when I was younger sitting down
with my parents, grandparents, and other relatives to enjoy a
delicious turkey dinner complete with all of the trimmings,
which included mincemeat and pumpkin pies.

We went to church the night before to give thanks to
God for the many blessings that we received during the year
and to pray for those people who were in need of His love
and attention.

Thanksgiving morning was fun because my brothers and
I could play football or basketball outside; or, if the weather
was bad, your great-grandfather took us bowling to enjoy a
few games before dinner and then we'd watch football on
television.

Thanksgiving was special to me because the people I
cared about the most came together to share a happy time,
and there were fun things to enjoy without having to worry
about the pressure of work or school. We were all in one

place and there was a sense of security and stability as we relished the holiday and the time we could spend with one another.

The celebration of Thanksgiving Day is almost four hundred years old now. When that first group of Pilgrims sailed across the Atlantic Ocean and in 1620 landed in what is now known as the state of Massachusetts, that first year was difficult for them. They partnered with the Iroquois Indians to learn how to grow corn and other crops as well as how to hunt and fish. In subsequent years they gathered once a year to celebrate the autumn harvest with a feast of thanks.

When the United States became an independent country, Congress recommended that our nation designate one annual day of Thanksgiving; it was Abraham Lincoln who suggested that Thanksgiving Day always be celebrated on the last Thursday of November.

While Thanksgiving Day only happens once a year, I wish that the spirit of Thanksgiving would penetrate the hearts of all people every day. "Thank you" is a phrase that I just don't hear as often as I did years ago. And yet, there is so much to be thankful for, even in these troubled times.

Be thankful, Ethan, for the God who created you and for the many blessings that He bestows upon you. Be thankful for your parents who brought you into this world and nurtured your growth and development. Be thankful for your family, your friends, your teachers, and those who share with you what is good in life. Be thankful for the opportunity to use your gifts and talents to make the world a better place. Be thankful for those challenging and humbling experiences that teach you how to rise above adversity and pain. Be thankful for your imperfections, understanding that no one is perfect and that God still loves us unconditionally and forever.

I know that you will find your own reasons to give thanks in your life. I hope that the gratitude you feel in your heart will always be expressed with a "Thank you" or a simple act of kindness that lightens another's burden or brings a smile to their face, not just on Thanksgiving Day, but every day.

I love you, Ethan.
Grandpa

EAR ETHAN:

If there is one virtue that has the power to change the character of humanity, respect is that virtue.

I frequently joke with people telling them that when I was younger I used to be an optimist, then I became a pessimist, and now in my senior years, I'm a realist. And, realistically speaking, I'm appalled today at the gradual disintegration of respect for life itself in our society.

Marriages are in jeopardy because husbands and wives fail to demonstrate respect for one another; families are experiencing crises because they neglect to nurture mutual respect; employees in virtually every industry are feeling more and more devalued; and finally, if you're a customer in today's marketplace, disrespect seems to be more the norm rather than the exception, despite the lofty platitudes we hear about service being so important.

I was flying to Detroit recently from Tampa and, while waiting to board the flight, the lack of respect I witnessed from an employee to a passenger was absolutely outrageous.

A young man in his mid-twenties was standing directly in front of me in line when he presented his boarding pass to the gate agent. The airline representative noticed that his luggage was too large for storage either in the overhead compartment or under the seat.

She glared at the passenger, took the bag from his hand, and said, "You're not allowed to bring this with you on the plane." Raising her voice and holding the luggage over the measuring compartment at the gate, she challenged him in a condescending fashion, "Can't you see that your luggage won't fit into this space? It will cost you twenty dollars to check this bag."

Unfortunately, when the young man confessed that he had a total of eight dollars in his pocket and no credit cards, the gate agent said, "Then you'll just have to go downstairs and re-book your flight. You should have known better." At that point about a half-dozen people, including me, offered to make up the difference and, thankfully, he was allowed to continue on to Detroit.

In retrospect, however, was the behavior of the gate agent really necessary? Not only did she disrespect the young man, but she embarrassed and humiliated him by raising her voice and making a scapegoat out of him in front of the one hundred and fifty people or so who were still waiting to board the aircraft.

Sad to say, that type of exchange happens too frequently

today and there is certainly no justification for it.

Respect, Ethan, has to be born inside of you. If you don't respect yourself, it's pretty difficult to demonstrate any level of respect for another human being.

However, when respect is the cornerstone of a relationship, there is seldom a goal that cannot be accomplished, an obstacle that cannot be overcome, or a bridge of understanding that cannot be constructed.

Occasionally, you'll hear a coach tell a reporter that he has no respect for his opponent. And in another interview a different coach will assert the opposite, claiming the greatest respect for the team that he is about to encounter.

It's been my observation that the coach possessing no respect is more often beaten while the respectful coach is more often victorious. Why does that happen? Simple. The coach demonstrating respect understands the task at hand, the skills and abilities of his opponent, and the specifics of what it takes to be victorious. In this instance, respect characterizes the framework for success. On the other hand, the coach who minimizes his regard for an opponent is a victim of arrogance and stupidity and, in most cases, loses the game.

Finally, Ethan, respect is not so much conforming to external rituals of behavior as it is the expression of an internal desire to fortify the sacredness of life.

But there's a very important key to earning the respect of your family, friends, and colleagues. And that is to employ one of the most energizing principles in all of behavioral science, which states that to the extent you give to others what they want, they will give to you what you want.

Respect isn't something that you wait to receive from another; rather, respect is a virtue that you rejoice in giving to those who hunger for it.

I love you, Ethan.
Grandpa

"If you're going through hell, keep going."

Winston Churchill

EAR ETHAN:

One of the inevitable realities of life is adversity. No matter how smoothly things seem to be going, adversity can punch you in the face and knock you down. Each one of us encounters challenges and obstacles that can cause minor inconvenience, ongoing frustration, and even chronic depression.

Unfortunately, our common perception of adversity is the professional golfer being interviewed on television who has just double-bogeyed the 18th hole of a major golf tournament that cost him the victory. Or we listen to the relief pitcher that blows the save in the seventh game of the World Series and his team loses the championship. Perhaps we learn about a CEO who misses his annual bonus due to a decrease in sales and market share or an employee whose reward trip gets cancelled because of a lack of funds in the budget.

Trust me. While these scenarios may be framed using the theme of adversity, they're not even close to the real deal.

Not long ago I had a colleague who attended a conference with me in the Midwest. Traveling home she experienced seizures on the plane, only later to find out that the diagnosis was inoperable brain cancer. That's adversity.

During my career as a marriage and family therapist I counseled a couple whose twelve-year-old daughter never came home from school one day. Extensive searches and investigations were unsuccessful in determining her whereabouts, and she was never heard from again. That's adversity.

A young soldier in our community, nineteen years old, left for Afghanistan in December, and in February his fellow soldiers carried his body from an airplane with a flag draped over the coffin. That's adversity.

Hopefully, Ethan, the adversity that you experience in your life will not be the kind that harms you physically or paralyzes you emotionally in a way that alters your life's destiny.

But when adversity does find you, these are just a few things you can do that might help you to manage the experience in a positive way and strengthen your character in the long term:

- ▶ Never give up. Be persistent in your resolve to understand, control, and overcome the hardships that confront you.

- ▶ Be patient. Maintain your calm and composure and believe that you have the strength to manage the situation with grace and dignity.

▶ Ask for help when you need it. Don't be ashamed to reach out to those who love you and care about you and those who want to stand beside you in your time of need.

▶ Remember that adversity is an experience that has a beginning and an end. Search for the light that's always at the end of the tunnel but may temporarily be invisible to you.

▶ Pray to God and ask for His help. I always felt that when I was in the worst of situations, God had His arm around my shoulder.

I remember a time when adversity had a firm grip on my own life. Even though everyone around me was celebrating the holidays, misery characterized my mood on a daily basis and I'm sure that I wasn't a fun person to be around.

One day when I arrived home from work, there was a single card waiting for me on the counter that I assumed was a Christmas card, so I threw it in the garbage can in our kitchen. A couple of hours later I felt a remorse for trashing someone's attempt to communicate with me and I went to retrieve the envelope.

It was in fact a Christmas card from an old friend that I hadn't heard from in years. He wrote a couple of lines saying that he remembered the good times we used to have and that he thought that I would enjoy the message on the front of the card.

I want to share the message with you, Ethan, and hope that you will always remember it in times of adversity.

Footprints in the Sand
(Mary Stevenson)

One night I dreamed I was walking
along the beach with the Lord.
Many scenes from my life flashed across the sky.
In each scene I noticed footprints in the sand.
Sometimes there were two sets of footprints,
Other times there was one set of footprints.

This bothered me because I noticed
That during the low periods in my life
When I was suffering from
Anguish, sorrow, or defeat,
I could see only one set of footprints.

So I said to the Lord,
"You promised me Lord,
That if I followed you,
You would walk with me always.
But I have noticed that during
The most trying periods of my life
There has been only one
Set of footprints in the sand.
Why, when I needed you most,
Have you not been there for me?"

The Lord replied,
"The times when you have
Seen only one set of footprints in the sand,
Is when I carried you."

I love you, Ethan.
Grandpa

 EAR ETHAN:

I was reading an article by a professor at UCLA who was describing that in the traditional villages of Fiji when people grow old, family and friends care for them until they die. In America, the elderly are more typically sent to nursing homes. The professor went on to articulate the commonly held thought that many societies treat their elderly better than Americans do. That's very sad.

There are several factors working against respect for the elderly in our country. Modern literacy, for example, with its affinity for technology, makes it easier to look things up in a book or on the Internet than to ask an old person. In addition, our Protestant work ethic implies that when a person retires and is no longer working that the individual has lost value in the eyes of society.

The fact of the matter is that our senior citizens have a wealth of experience and wisdom that can benefit young people in virtually every dimension of their lives.

In addition, if we took a close look at history, closing the book on old people when they retire is a terrible mistake given their record of accomplishing extraordinary things later in life.

No one can ever forget the tremendous accomplishments of the civil rights activist Rosa Parks who died at ninety-two after a lifetime of advancing the cause of civil rights in America. The famous news reporter Walter Cronkite died at the age of ninety-two but always regretted retiring as the CBS news anchor at the youthful age of sixty-five; and retired US Senator John Glenn became the oldest man in space at seventy-seven. And who can forget Mother Teresa who died at the age of eighty-seven and spent over forty-five years ministering to the sick, orphaned, poor, and dying?

Rosa Parks, Walter Cronkite, John Glenn, and Mother Teresa are all examples of famous individuals who achieved great things well into their senior years. But what we'll never know, Ethan, are the countless numbers of older people from families throughout America who are contributing to a better world on a daily basis with little or no recognition of any kind.

And one of those people is your great-grandmother Marie, who at the age of ninety is still adding to her 7,000 hours of volunteer work at St. Elizabeth Medical Center by working with a group of women there to make "heart pillows" for patients who have undergone cardiac care. The "pillow ladies," as they are affectionately known, bring their healing ministry to patients who will never meet them or know them.

Several presidents of the United States have repeatedly told us that children are our country's greatest natural resource. There is no question as to the veracity of that statement. What I would say, however, is that senior citizens are our country's greatest treasure. And they are a treasure that we have not fully appreciated or valued in terms of their ability to make a positive and meaningful impact upon our society.

I'm beginning to experience the realities of growing old. I've worked on a consulting project for the past fourteen years with the same company. During that time I've seen many younger people awarded contracts to work on the same project, many of them young enough to be my children. With all of the experience I've acquired the hard way and the wealth of information I have that could make their jobs a lot easier—unless I volunteer useful information, which I frequently do—I'm seldom asked for an opinion or an idea by my younger colleagues.

I hope that as you grow older you will seek out the wisdom of those who have been there and done that; taking that initiative will certainly shorten your learning curve while providing you with valuable information that will complement what you already know.

There's no substitute for experience. Knowledge is great, training is wonderful, and passion for what you do can go a long way in the pursuit of your dreams. But those who are in the autumn and the winter of their lives here on earth can enlighten your path, and their experiences can infuse you with a wealth of insight that will enrich your life personally and professionally.

So I hope that you will always respect those who have gone before you. We've all made mistakes; we've all had our share of failures; and we don't know all of the answers. What matters most, however, is not so much the outcome we experienced in our own lives but the wisdom that you can derive from our journeys.

I love you, Ethan.
Grandpa

> "Many persons have a wrong idea of
> what constitutes true happiness.
> It is not attained through self-gratification
> but through fidelity to a worthy cause."
>
> Helen Keller

DEAR ETHAN:

If I heard it once, I heard it a thousand times: "I'm just not happy." Those were the words of people who came to my office for counseling because they were feeling discouraged and depressed.

They weren't unhappy because their favorite team lost a game or because traffic was particularly bad on a given day. They were most often frustrated because their concept of happiness was one that could never be realized in this life.

The fundamental problem with perpetually unhappy people is that they perceive happiness as an emotion that they need to feel rather than a way of life that they have the opportunity to live.

It's interesting that research studies on generational happiness indicate that senior citizens are happier than the young. While older people report more health problems, their level of contentment surpassed those younger people who struggled with marital, financial, and career stress.

While I believe in the sociological results of that research, I feel that there's a more significant explanation for the researcher's conclusions. From my own perspective, I came to the realization some time ago that the attainment of material possessions and wealth was not consistent with the message that I shared with you in an earlier letter about the real purpose for life.

As I've aged and had the opportunity to live out that purpose—to know people, engage people, and uplift people—I've experienced genuine happiness.

Oh sure, I'm happy when the Tampa Bay Lightning win a hockey game. I'm happy when I get to visit our family in New York. And I'm happy when I can share good times with my colleagues and friends. There are a lot of things that give me that emotional satisfaction one would associate with happiness. And there's certainly nothing wrong with enjoying those feelings whenever we can experience them.

But what happens when the hockey team loses, my trip gets cancelled, or my colleagues and friends disappoint me? I'm certainly not happy.

So I'm sure you can understand, Ethan, just how frustrating it would be to rely upon a series of external events that make us feel happy one day and frustrated the next for our entire lives.

And that is why there is a different type of happiness that I hope you find in your lifetime, a happiness that never ends. That happiness is founded in the reality that God created you for a purpose, and because He did, your life had meaning before it even began.

Practically speaking, should you come to embrace the belief that we are put on this earth to know people, engage people, and uplift the lives of others, and then act upon that belief, you will experience a permanent happiness in the very depths of your heart and soul.

Some time ago I discovered an old Chinese proverb that summarizes my thinking about happiness:

If you want happiness for an hour, take a nap.

If you want happiness for a day, go fishing.

If you want happiness for a year, inherit a fortune.

If you want happiness for a lifetime, help someone else.

A great example of that Chinese proverb is George Washington Carver, and I hope that you learn about his extraordinary life in history class one day.

Mr. Carver was born in Missouri in 1864 as a slave. He and his mother were abducted by slave raiders when he was an infant and later his Mom was sold while his master bought him back in exchange for a horse.

By the time he was thirteen years old he was on his own. He got a job working on a farm and found a way to obtain his high school education. Later he became the first Negro student ever admitted to Simpson College in Iowa where he worked as a janitor to pay for his education.

After receiving his master's degree, he was hired by Booker T. Washington to head the agriculture department at the Tuskegee Institute in Alabama where he spent the rest of his life enhancing their laboratory and doing research.

George Washington Carver was an exceptional human

being. He strengthened the economy of the South by discovering that nitrogen-producing legumes, peanuts, and sweet potatoes improved the soil. In order to give the farmers a reason for planting those crops, he created over three hundred byproducts and taught the farmers how to enrich their land.

In terms of experiencing the happiness that comes from knowing, engaging, and uplifting people's lives, Mr. Carver was a perfect role model. While he made many discoveries as a part of his research, he refused to patent any of them. He was quoted as saying, "God gave them to me. How can I sell them to someone else?"

Before his death in 1943, he donated $30,000 of his savings to the George Washington Carver Foundation and willed that organization the balance of his estate so that his work would be continued after his death. Fittingly, his epitaph read: "He could have added fortune to fame, but caring for neither, he found happiness and honor in being helpful to the world."

For as long as I live, Ethan, I will pray that you enjoy the happiness and joy that comes from those everyday moments that we treasure with our family and friends. But, most importantly, I'm going to ask God to guide you in the path of that inner happiness and contentment that finds us when we live our lives in a manner similar to George Washington Carver.

I love you, Ethan.
Grandpa

"To lead the people, walk behind them."

Lao-Tzu

DEAR ETHAN:

I believe that anyone who reads this letter in the future, knowing the time that it was written, would have to agree that we experienced a poverty of leadership in our country at the beginning of the twenty-first century.

The news media salivates as they wait for the next scandal to rock the world of politics, religion, or business. Employees bemoan a lack of trust and integrity among their managers. And even children are increasingly confused today at the mixed messages that they receive from their parents who demand adherence to a set of strict behavioral standards while compromising their own sense of right and wrong all too often.

It's way too easy to blame our struggling economy, unemployment, terrorism, and a host of other concerns for the lack of leadership that we experience today. But none of that matters really. Every generation has been faced with problems that seem insurmountable at the time but their foundation of leadership was fundamentally strong and they managed those problems effectively and efficiently.

What's changed about contemporary leadership in my opinion is that we seem to have drifted away from the core vision and values that made our country great. Greed permeates our culture and complacency has weakened our standing among the nations of the world.

I'm going to pray from now until the day I die that two things happen as your generation takes the reins and shapes America's identity.

First, all human beings need to understand that leadership is part of their character and destiny. No, not everyone is meant to be a CEO or president of the United States, but the most effective leadership is not always characterized by formal roles and responsibilities.

You will be a well-respected leader, Ethan, when you lead by example. Doing the right thing doesn't require that you hold an office or receive executive compensation. No formal education is necessary to demonstrate honesty, compassion, integrity, or helpfulness. Leading by example may sound like a timeworn phrase and an old-fashioned idea, but nothing can compare with its synergy in generating collaboration and cooperation among people from every walk of life.

Look no further than your pediatrician and our family friend, Dr. Dean Fauber, as an example of someone who leads by example. For many years, Dean, his wife, MaryAnne, and their family have made numerous trips to Haiti to treat children who would otherwise be without medical care and treatment. Their example as a family inspired others to become a part of this ministry and they were able to save many lives during their missionary trips.

The Faubers are leaders in the compassion they demonstrate for humanity.

Secondly, making the Golden Rule the cornerstone of our personal conduct will change the face of a culture whose diminishing respect for human life is frightening.

"Do unto others as you would have them do unto you" is a phrase that can be found in virtually every religion. I remember when I was in grammar school seeing those words written in big, bold letters on Mrs. Moore's blackboard in our fifth grade classroom. Then in religion class we talked about what those words meant in our day-to-day lives. Somehow I missed the main message.

I used to think that the Golden Rule meant that if someone was nice to me then I should be nice to them in return. Or if someone reached out to help me then I would return the favor when they needed assistance. No, that's not what "Do unto others as you would have them do unto you" really means.

Maybe if I paid a little more attention in class I would have seen that the Golden Rule begins with a verb and that it doesn't contain any conditions or clauses. In fact, living the Golden Rule means being the first to do the right thing and to treat others in a way that dignifies their heritage as children of God.

Oh, there's a lot of risk in being true to the Golden Rule. Your attempts to take the initiative to help others can be met with indifference and rejection. But for every failed attempt to have your good will accepted and reciprocated, you will be richly blessed by those who embrace your kindness, help, and friendship.

Cynics will laugh at the simplicity and the naiveté of being the first to treat people the way you want to be treated. Don't be fooled, Ethan. Those will be the same people who complain about the way things are and then criticize others who offer solutions to make things better.

Leadership isn't a collection of complex theories and management styles. Leadership implies a keen awareness of our identity as children of God, combined with a realization that our mission in this world is to serve the needs of our brothers and sisters in whatever location and vocation we find ourselves.

Of course, the idea of a servant leader sounds contradictory but, in reality, it is the essence of what genuine leadership is all about. Servant leadership characterized the ministry of Jesus Christ when He walked on this earth and, rather than receive public acclaim for anything that He did, Jesus was often heard asking His followers not to tell anyone.

And so, Ethan, you may never be elected president, governor, or mayor. You may never captain a ship or lead a sports team onto the field. But you can still be one of the most legendary leaders in history when you lead by a good example and when you take the first step in treating others the way you want to be treated. And you can rest assured that your reward will be greater than any earthly prize or recognition when you get to heaven.

I love you, Ethan.
Grandpa

$\mathscr{D}$EAR ETHAN:

Tonight I was giving you your bottle before bedtime and
we were just sitting together quietly while your Mom and
Dad enjoyed a well-deserved date night. You were content,
peaceful, and ready for a good night's sleep after a fun-
filled evening at Chuck E. Cheese's.

As we sat there together, knowing how secure you
were in my arms, I couldn't help but think of the potential
dangers that you would have to face in the years to come
when I wouldn't be able to hold you, advise you, or protect
you.

It's frightening to think about all of the pitfalls that
lurk along the path of life, especially for kids growing up.
And perhaps the most insidious of all evils is the threat of
alcohol and drug abuse.

I've counseled and consoled my share of weeping and
sobbing parents over the years whose children were either

alcoholics, drug addicts, or both. Alcohol and drugs are in schools, parties, on the street, in clubs and most places where kids congregate. Preteens and teenagers don't have to look too far to find alcohol and drugs; most often, alcohol and drugs find them.

No one will ever understand just how tragic it is or the severity of the emotional, gut-wrenching pain that parents suffer when they lose a child to substance abuse. And the statistics are alarming, even after all these years of education and public awareness campaigns.

Alcohol, for example, is still a leading cause of death among youth, particularly teenagers, as it contributes substantially to adolescent motor vehicle crashes, other traumatic injuries, suicide, date rape, and family and school problems.

What most young people don't realize, Ethan, is that one mistake, one bad decision, or one error in judgment as a result of being under the influence of alcohol or drugs can be a point of no return when it comes to losing a friend, a career, and even a life.

Young people abuse alcohol and drugs for one of two basic reasons; first, their sense of self-esteem hasn't been developed sufficiently and they feel a need to medicate themselves from the pain of their own perceived unworthiness; and secondly, they can't manage the peer pressure of their friends and acquaintances who want them to identify with a particular group or lifestyle.

When I was growing up my parents taught me how to

drink responsibly. At Thanksgiving and special occasions we'd have wine on the table for dinner, and as I grew older I'd occasionally share a drink with my family at a special event or gathering. But thankfully, I never saw alcohol as a remedy for life's frustrations and never thought so little of myself that I needed to drink or use drugs in order to feel welcome in a particular group or clique.

During my freshman year in college I met a great guy named Jake in one of my classes. We had some things in common and also played on the same intramural sports teams during the spring and fall semesters.

Jake had a very beautiful girlfriend that he had known since high school who attended a neighboring engineering college. I would say she was the type of girl who lived on the edge and was a risk-taking person to the extreme point where her behavior sometimes bordered on the reckless and dangerous. Jake and Trish were together frequently. They were a bit of an odd couple in that she drank, he didn't; she experimented with marijuana, he didn't; she was going to be an engineer, and he was a jock who wanted to play sports and get a marketing degree after he retired from his professional baseball career.

Jake called me up one day and it was obvious he had been drinking. He was crying and upset because Trish had severed the relationship and found another boyfriend who she said she "identified with" more than Jake.

My friend was devastated and broken-hearted. Although he had dated some in early high school, Jake and Trish had been together for the past three years. It seems as though he had been in denial about her substance abuse issues and always thought that she would see the light one day and that he would be there for her when she did.

As much as I tried to be there to talk Jake through this loss, nothing seemed to help. He wouldn't seek the advice of a counselor, viewed himself as the reason Trish left, and became more despondent as the weeks and months passed. He continued to drink, missed classes, lost his academic scholarship, and eventually dropped out of school and went back to the Midwest to find a job.

Not long ago I found Jake on a social networking site on the Internet after forty years of not having contact with him. He's still in the Midwest working as a customer service representative for a large telephone network. "For a while," he said, "I blamed Trish and alcohol for me winding up in a rehabilitation center and losing a promising baseball career. Then I realized one day that I had only myself to answer for. I didn't really know myself back in those days. Life then was about doing great things and playing great games and getting a lot of recognition for my baseball skills. But understanding who I really was on the inside, and learning about how to manage relationships and life, well, that was my downfall."

Jake's story has a lesson in it for all of us, Ethan. The answer to a personal crisis or a relationship problem isn't found in a bottle, a needle, or a pill.

When bad things happen in life, we have to call upon

the inner strength and courage that God gives us to manage those situations to the best of our ability, reach out to those who can offer guidance and help, and rely upon our intellect, emotions, and will to persevere, overcome the crisis, and emerge in the aftermath with our values, dignity, and self-respect intact.

I love you, Ethan.
Grandpa

> "Human progress is neither automatic nor
> inevitable ... Every step toward the goal of
> justice requires sacrifice, suffering, and struggle;
> the tireless exertions and passionate
> concern of dedicated individuals."
>
> Martin Luther King Jr.

 EAR ETHAN:

I want to tell you a story about a word that's seldom heard in our society today and that word is sacrifice. Unlike the old days when sacrifice described a worship offering to the gods, today's metaphorical meaning suggests the act of performing selfless good deeds for others, or a short-term loss in return for a greater long-term gain.

Parents, for example, often times sacrifice their own wants and needs for the sake of providing some benefit or good to their children. A young couple might sacrifice the joys of a lavish honeymoon to begin saving money for their life together. A daughter will sacrifice a promotion and a promising career to stay in her hometown and care for her ailing parents. Or, a homeless person with only one coat to shelter himself from the cold will sacrifice his comfort to a friend who has nothing to wear.

Whatever the situation, making a sacrifice to help a family member, friend, or worthy cause is the lifeblood of a healthy society. Sacrifice is the antidote to selfishness. And in an era which glorifies self-satisfaction, self-aggrandizement, and self-absorption, we need the dose of reality that sacrifice brings to get back to the real work of building a better world.

What's really interesting, Ethan, is that the things that I thought would bring me the most satisfaction in life were not that rewarding when I actually acquired them or experienced them. Whether the things that I sought were tangible or intangible made no difference.

On the other hand, as I look back on my life now after all these years, I can see clearly that anytime I found myself in a position to make a sacrifice for a person or an ideal that mattered, my sense of self-worth and personal satisfaction seemed to be enriched a hundredfold.

Not only that, the positive results associated with successfully undertaking my sacrifice produced a sense of personal well-being that far outlasted the happiness I had experienced in acquiring any material possession or in receiving any gift.

There is a story about a young boy whose big brother sustained significant injuries in an automobile crash. Shortly after the accident, the youngster's dad approached him and said, "Trent, I need to ask you something very important.

Your brother needs a blood transfusion in order to live. And the doctors at the hospital have determined that only you have the special type of blood that matches your brother's. Will you help your brother so that he might live?"

Without hesitation, Trent wanted to help his brother. He had no idea that the procedure itself was generally simple and safe and that it posed no threat to his life.

On the way to the hospital, Trent was unusually quiet while his father found himself in the most awkward and uncomfortable position of his life. Because he didn't want to create any additional anxiety for his younger son, he kept his thoughts to himself.

Within minutes they were at the front door of the Blake Regional Medical Center and went to Trent's brother's room. As they entered, the nurse was there waiting with a needle. She sat Trent down, remarked at how courageous he was for wanting to help his big brother, and told him not to worry because she had done this a hundred times before.

As she inserted the needle into his arm the blood began to fill the vial slowly. After the vial filled, Trent, with tears in his eyes, turned to his father and said, "Daddy, how long do I have now before I die?"

Not surprisingly, young children are willing to sacrifice their lives to save someone they love. Those who have been the closest to God most recently seem to be infused with that sacrificial love that caused Him to give us his only Son so that we might have eternal life.

As we get older, life gets cluttered with our personal

possessions and material things, which cloud our sense of sacrifice. As you mature, Ethan, I hope that you will come to understand that what you sacrifice for the good of others may never be recognized or remembered in this life, but will most certainly be rewarded in the next.

I love you, Ethan.
Grandpa

"As you walk down the fairway of
life you must smell the roses, for you
only get to play one round."

Ben Hogan

EAR ETHAN:

I was in a meeting the other day with a group of young
executives. They were bemoaning their schedules and the
limited time they had to spend with their families or to have
any fun. In the middle of the conversation one of them said,
"I'm going to work until it's time to retire and then I'm
going to enjoy myself." Upon hearing that statement, his
co-workers grudgingly nodded in agreement.

Life can take its toll on the human spirit, Ethan. With
the pressures of work, family obligations, health concerns,
and financial pressures, our day-to-day responsibilities can
make us feel like we're merely struggling to survive rather
than experiencing any personal or professional satisfaction
and fulfillment.

So it's important as you go through life to find a balance,
a balance that enables you to have fun and to enjoy your
family and friends. Having fun doesn't always cost money.

When I was growing up we didn't have a lot of extra cash for vacations and trips but we always found things to do that brought smiles to our faces and joy to our hearts.

I remember as a kid having a basketball hoop in our backyard attached to the garage and I would often be found outside after school playing with my brothers and the other kids in the neighborhood. It was fun imagining that we were Wilt Chamberlain, Bill Russell, Jerry West, and the other NBA stars in those days; our games took the pressure off schoolwork and the other responsibilities that kids shoulder during their developmental years.

Sometimes on a Sunday our family would take a drive in the car to nearby Sylvan Beach, go for a swim, and enjoy the rides and cotton candy in the small amusement park there. We had fun, forgot all about school, cleaning our rooms, and other tasks that could wait at least until the next day.

During college when I was working in the summer to help pay for some academic expenses and earning spending money at the same time, I enjoyed attending a few summer concerts at the Saratoga Performing Arts Center. Sitting in the cheap seats on the grass, it was relaxing to listen to the sounds of James Taylor, Carole King, The Rolling Stones, and Peter, Paul & Mary with my college friends. Nothing could have been more wonderful than the sound of that music or sharing the company of people that I enjoyed.

When I became a parent, fun for me was coaching your Dad's baseball team. I wouldn't trade a minute for the times we spent together driving to practice or getting an ice cream or a Coke after the game. And for most summers we'd travel back to visit family and friends in upstate New York and your Dad had an opportunity to enjoy his grandmother, aunts, uncles, and cousins.

Now, my fun is hanging out with you, Ethan, and I hope that I'm blessed with many more years to enjoy you, laugh and learn with you, and share some of those special times that grandfathers spend with their grandsons. Oh, I threaten your Mom and Dad that if I didn't have a job I'd be at your house everyday because there are really no words that can adequately describe the joy that fills my heart when I have the opportunity to see you and spend time with you.

So looking back over the years, our family never owned a super-sized yacht to take us to exotic places; we never had a summer home where we could escape for the winter; and as my mother would customarily say, we never lived in the "lap of luxury." But somehow growing up I always managed to have fun doing things with family and friends, and that tradition continues with you today.

While work and family responsibilities are important, Ethan, I want you always to remember to make the time to have fun and relax alone and with your friends and family. Go to the gym, play a round of golf, watch a baseball game, or walk a couple of miles. Find something that brings you a little peace and contentment and make it a part of your regular routine.

It's not a good thing that the pace of life has increased so dramatically in our society since I was a child. I'm sorry to say that being too busy has caused me to forfeit time that would have been better spent having fun on more occasions than I care to acknowledge. Please don't make the same mistake.

Have fun!

I love you, Ethan.

Grandpa

> "A rock pile ceases to be a rock pile the
> moment a single man contemplates it,
> bearing within him the image of a cathedral."
>
> Antoine de Saint-Exuperey

EAR ETHAN:

One of the greatest untapped resources in a person's life is his imagination. There's no limit to what your imagination can conceive. Most people don't even understand the significance of their imagination and its creative power. Parents, schools, and businesses don't pay enough attention to what can be done to develop the potential of a human being.

And, interestingly enough, our imagination is the tool that we use to encounter everything in life. The things that we see, hear, and touch form a picture through the lens of our imagination. Simply stated, our imagination is the capacity to form mental images, sensations, and concepts at a time when they haven't yet been perceived through sight, hearing, or senses.

Imagination is the vehicle that provides meaning to experience, and understanding to knowledge. Imagination is the way we make sense of what is happening in the world and it is a key factor in the learning process. Unfortunately, I think that the power of the imagination scares some people who prefer a regimented, orderly, left-brain world and who would rather enjoy the predictable rather than to create what is possible in life.

When you read your history books and take a trip to Orlando, Florida, Ethan, you'll learn about one of the world's greatest imagineers, Walt Disney. It was Walt who said, "All our dreams can come true if we have the courage to pursue them." And if you're fortunate enough to experience Walt's dream, Disney World, you'll see for yourself what the imagination can create and the joy that it can bring to countless numbers of people year after year.

When Albert Einstein said that "Imagination is more important than knowledge," he certainly rocked a few boats in the world of academics and higher learning. But the untold numbers of real-life examples of Einstein's assertion are powerfully convincing.

One of those true stories is of Air Force Colonel George Hall. Colonel Hall was captured during the Vietnam War and placed in solitary confinement for seven torturous years. In order to survive, he played a round of golf in his imagination every day. One week after his release from that POW camp he played golf for real in the Greater New Orleans Open and shot a 76, an incredible golf score under the circumstances.

Another powerful testimony to the imagination is that of Dr. Vera Fryling. During the Holocaust she was on the run from the Gestapo while living undercover in Berlin. To pass the time while she was in hiding, she imagined that she was a psychiatrist living in a free country and helping others.

Dr. Fryling subsequently escaped the Nazis, the Soviet Army, and overcame a battle with cancer to find herself on the faculty of the San Francisco Medical School. In one of her comments about the ordeal, she said, "Imagination can help one transcend the insults life has dealt us."

While Colonel Hall's and Dr. Fryling's stories are famous examples of the powers of the imagination, it's important to know that you have those same abilities, Ethan.

As you grow up, there are a few things that you can do to strengthen the power of your imagination:

▶ Be curious about everything. There are so many amazing wonders in the world for you to learn about and experience. In your exploration you will create a bank of memories and ideas that you can use as you need them.

▶ When you're faced with problems or obstacles, use your imagination to identify several ways to resolve the issue rather than just employing the usual approach.

▶ As you develop your interests and talents, brainstorm opportunities to expand them and learn as much as you can. Ask questions, talk to the experts in your field, and look for ways to improve and build upon the ideas of others.

▶ There isn't much that doesn't need improvement. Be on the lookout for innovations that could use a fresh idea or a better process. Think outside the box and interact with creative people in search of a new outlook or approach.

▶ Commit yourself to generating a couple of creative ideas each week. I guarantee you that by the end of one year you'll have at least a dozen that will positively impact your life or the lives of others. Give yourself permission to be creative.

Solutions to the problems that face our nation, cures for the diseases that plague us, and remedies for our most subtle and profound concerns can be found by employing the power of our imagination.

I hope that you embrace this tremendous resource, Ethan. God has given you the special gift of imagination, and I pray that you will use it to experience the fullness of life and as a tool to enrich the lives of others.

I love you, Ethan.
Grandpa

DEAR ETHAN:

There's a two-step process that would foster peace, harmony, and healing throughout the world. It's a process that's frequently used when there's a massive crisis at hand, but implemented less frequently in our everyday interactions.

If empathizing with another's pain or misfortune and then acting compassionately to help remedy that pain or misfortune became the behavioral norm for people all over the world, our lives would be enriched beyond measure.

When a catastrophic earthquake struck Haiti in 2010, which resulted in an estimated 200,000 deaths and 300,000 injuries, the outpouring of empathy and compassion from around the world was phenomenal. In addition to the massive relief efforts that were coordinated among twenty or more countries, there were untold stories of individuals and small groups who left their spouses, families, and jobs to minister to the needs of the Haitian people. To witness that selfless outpouring of empathy and compassion on the part of the world community was truly heartening.

On the other side of the coin, I was talking to a woman in her seventies recently who had been temporarily disabled and couldn't leave the house to buy groceries, and neither her son nor three neighbors in her development were willing to shop for her or take her to the supermarket.

The testimony of positive change in the world and the power of empathy and compassion are most certainly evidenced in the massive relief efforts that we witnessed during the Haitian disaster. But the true character of empathy and compassion is developed one act of kindness at a time within the framework of our own lives

What's amazing, Ethan, is that empathy and compassion can be witnessed most often in the lives of God's youngest children. I remember when you were just about a year old and you sat in your high chair for lunch while I was sitting next to you. You'd grab a piece of fruit from your plate and hold it out for me to eat with a big grin on your face.

As a matter of fact, whenever we were at a meal together at your house or a restaurant, I might ask you for a vegetable or a little applesauce and without fail, you would push some food from your plate in my direction. No one teaches a newborn empathy and compassion, yet younger children seem to be the most likely to demonstrate those traits.

There was a famous author who was invited to judge a contest to find the most caring child. It turns out that the winner was a four-year-old whose elderly neighbor had just lost his wife of many years. One day Kyle, the contest winner, saw the man outside on his porch just sitting there and crying. Kyle's mother saw her son go over to the man and jump up on his lap. He sat there for a while and when he came back home his mother asked him what he had said to their neighbor. "Nothing, Mommy," Kyle said. "I just helped him cry."

It's only when we get older that selfishness and cynicism get in the way and the presence of empathy and compassion diminishes.

The old maxim of "seek first to understand and then to be understood" is the foundation of people who demonstrate empathy on a routine basis. And it's that empathetic understanding that sparks the fire of compassionate acts that have the power to heal broken spirits and mend shattered hearts.

Governments literally spend millions of dollars on cultural studies trying to determine how to achieve a more peaceful world and additional research on how to avoid conflicts and wars. They look for ways that world communities might construct bridges of peace and understanding while minimizing international hostilities. The trouble is that too often we opt to search for the complex cures rather than to discover the wisdom of simple solutions.

Anyone who has bestowed the gifts of empathy and compassion on others has experienced the true meaning of being a living hope and help in this world. And anyone who has been the recipient of empathy and compassion has seen the face of God in their time of need.

As you grow up, Ethan, I hope that you embrace empathy and compassion as valuable gifts to make your life a more fulfilling and rewarding experience.

I love you, Ethan.
Grandpa

"Not to forgive is to be imprisoned by the past,
by old grievances that do not let life proceed
with new business. Not to forgive is to yield
oneself to another's control ... to be locked into
a sequence of act and response ... of outrage and
revenge, tit for tat, escalating always. The present
is endlessly overwhelmed and devoured by the
past. Forgiveness frees the forgiver. It extracts
the forgiver from someone else's nightmare."

Lance Morrow

$\mathcal{D}$EAR ETHAN:

Forgiveness is one of the most courageous acts that any human being can undertake in life. It's not something for the weak, only for the strong. The power of forgiveness can change the course of human relationships and history itself.

I want to tell you a true story about forgiveness, Ethan, a story that will most likely amaze you, puzzle you, and leave you wondering why. Nevertheless, the story that I'm about to share with you represents only a microcosm of a multitude of events that beg forgiveness throughout the world.

On a Monday morning in October of 2006, a group of Amish students went to their one-room school in the small town of Nickel Mines, Pennsylvania. Little did they know when they woke up that morning that a thirty-two-year-old gunman named Charles Roberts would enter their class of twenty-five pupils and then order the teachers and boys to leave the building.

After they had departed, Roberts tied the legs of the remaining ten girls and prepared to execute them with over four hundred rounds of ammunition that he brought with him to the school. The oldest of the girls begged the gunman to shoot her first while sparing the lives of the younger children. Her plea fell upon deaf ears and Roberts proceeded to open fire, killing five and leaving the rest critically wounded.

And what was the reason that Roberts gave for the massacre at Nickel Pines? Before he began shooting, and eventually turning the gun on himself, he said that he was angry at God for taking the life of his young daughter.

In the aftermath of the shootings, the small Pennsylvania town became saturated with news media from all over the United States and throughout the world. The fifty-plus news crews remained for the five days until both the killer and the children were buried.

Shortly after the perpetration of this heinous and unthinkable crime, the Amish parents offered words of forgiveness to the family of the man who had murdered their children.

To people on the outside, it was incredulous that the

families could offer forgiveness to their children's killer so soon after the crime. When interviews were conducted about the incident, the number of questions concerning the forgiveness expressed by the families far outnumbered any inquiries about the killer or the violent nature of the crime itself.

It was equally stunning that coming from the funerals of their children, the Amish families accounted for over half of the approximately seventy-five people who attend Roberts' burial. And not only did they greet his widow and her three children with compassion, their sense of forgiveness caused them to support a fund for the killer's family as well.

The story leaves us with many questions about how the Amish families were able to forgive so quickly. What was it about their religious beliefs and practices that kept their lives from being completely decimated by grief, and what does it mean for us and how we conduct our lives?

Of course, we probably don't need to look any further than the example of Jesus Christ. In keeping with His consistent message of unconditional love and forgiveness for all, as He hung on the cross, the first of His ten last words were, "Father, forgive them, for they know not what they do."

And, on another occasion in His ministry when He was asked by Peter the apostle if he should forgive someone who sins against him seven times, Jesus replied, "Not seven times I tell you, but seventy times seven."

There have been people in my life who have caused me harm both intentionally and unintentionally. In some cases, I hurt myself by not following the example of those Amish families and, more importantly, the example of Jesus Himself, and my act of forgiveness toward them was either delayed or, more shamefully, non-existent. I don't want you to make that same mistake.

One of the great realities of forgiveness, Ethan, is that it does not refer only to the absolution of guilt from things past. No, much more powerfully, forgiveness implies a restoration process that rebuilds relationships, families, and communities in the present and the future. And it is in that rebuilding that forgiveness both heals and strengthens us.

My message to you, Ethan, is that if you have been injured or harmed by the acts of another, remember that forgiveness is as important as anything you can think of doing to lessen the pain and the hurt. And if you have done something to harm another, asking for forgiveness can trigger a renewal that will make you whole again.

I love you, Ethan.
Grandpa

> "Don't pray when it rains if you don't
> pray when the sun shines."
>
> Satchel Paige

EAR ETHAN:

It may take you many years to fully understand what I'm
going to share with you now, but I know that when you
do you will have discovered one of life's most valuable
resources.

When I was a child I was taught very early about the
importance of praying to God. Of course, growing up
Catholic we were taught to recite the "Our Father," "Hail
Mary," and "Act of Contrition" among the many beautiful
prayers that expressed important messages about our faith
and our lives.

While not everyone prays or believes in the importance
of prayer, you will hear consistent references to it as you
grow up. A friend may ask you to pray for a sick relative,
or a news commentator will say, "Our prayers are with the
family during this difficult time." Before a football game
the announcer may ask the crowd to pause in silent prayer
to mourn the loss of a former player or owner.

One of my lessons in life has been to come to a simple

understanding of what prayer really is, and for me prayer is a conversation with God. I see communicating through prayer as my connection with heaven and the God who loves me. And the wonderful reality of prayer is that God has assured us that He listens when we communicate with Him.

But I'm certain that if we polled God on the types of prayers that He was hearing, the overwhelming majority of them would be prayers of petition. "God, please give me the wisdom to pass my chemistry test." "God, my mother-in-law is driving me crazy ... can't you do something?" "God, I really need some patience to help me deal with my nagging boss."

Whether it's peace of mind, patience, or prosperity, people reach out to God in prayer for a multitude of reasons. I know that I've prayed to God countless numbers of times in my life asking Him for an assortment of favors. What makes me sad is the number of times that my petitions were answered, yet my prayers of thanksgiving for God's goodness and grace were either slow in being said or completely forgotten.

As I've grown older, my prayers still include prayers of petition and thanksgiving, but limiting prayer to those two categories dramatically impairs its power. There are beautiful and meaningful prayers to adore God, praise Him, and celebrate the wonders of His creation.

But I keep retuning to my reality that prayer is a one-to-one, heart-to-heart talk with God. And while I do a fair amount of the speaking in our silent conversations, I recall my parents and grandparents encouraging me to listen for God speaking to me.

I had a close friend recently who was seeking a promotion at work that would have highlighted a wonderful career as an accountant in a prestigious firm. He wasn't selected for the advancement. When we were speaking the other day he was telling me how hard he had prayed to God for the promotion. I could sense a little bitterness in his voice as he said, "Yeah, and God must have been sleeping and not heard my prayers."

Oh, no, God wasn't sleeping or off-duty. The fact of the matter is that sometimes when we think that our prayers aren't being answered, they're being answered. And the fundamental premise for any prayer of petition should be that God's will be done, not ours.

So when you pray, Ethan, I hope that you always know that God never turns a deaf ear to you or to your prayers. He listens, understands your need, and for reasons known only to Him, responds in a way that manifests His will to you.

One of the prayers that helped me to understand the nature of God's response to our petitions was given to me many years ago on a card that was intended to console me after one of life's disappointments:

> I asked God for strength that I might achieve.
> I was made weak that I might learn humbly to obey. I asked for health that I might do greater things. I was given infirmity that I might do better things. I asked for riches that I might be happy. I was given poverty that I might be wise.

I asked for power that I might have the praise of men. I was given weakness that I might feel the need of God. I asked for all things that I might enjoy life. I was given life that I might enjoy all things. I got nothing that I asked for, but everything I hoped for. Almost despite myself, my unspoken prayers were answered. I am, among all men, most richly blessed.

My prayer for you, Ethan, is that you have many conversations with God throughout your life. And if you do, you will never be alone in this world. God will always be with you, ready to listen to you and reveal His will to you.

I love you, Ethan.
Grandpa

"Nothing in life is to be feared.
It is only to be understood."

Marie Curie

$\mathscr{D}$EAR ETHAN:

People are sometimes paralyzed by fear. It grips their lives and won't let go. At least that's what they think.

I've listened to all types of fears over the years and I've had more than a few of my own. Some people are afraid to talk in front of a group of people, while others are petrified at the thought of dying. Parents are fearful that their children will associate with the wrong group of kids and get into drugs. Describe just about any situation and someone has already attached a fear to the experience, even if the nature of the experience is positive.

"I'm afraid to swim in the pool because I might catch a disease." "I'm afraid to fly because the plane might crash." "I'm afraid to take my driving test because I might fail." And the list is never-ending.

One of the greatest acronyms for fear that I've ever heard is this: FEAR is False Education Appearing Real. That explanation works for me. Too often we delude ourselves into believing that a horrible outcome is just around the proverbial corner and the heart begins to race, the palms get sweaty, and the anxiety level increases dramatically.

Even if there was a real and concrete obstacle that stood in our way, the emotional energy that fear zaps out of the individual prohibits any meaningful effort to overcome that obstacle in a constructive fashion. Everyone pays the price for fear's reckless destruction.

When individuals and families came to me for counseling, fear would inevitably be a part of our discussion at some point. Often people would raise their eyebrows when I suggested to them that healthy fear was very motivating and that it should always be a part of their lives.

And there is a very clear line that separates healthy fear from harmful fear. I want my child to fear crossing the street without looking. I want my best friend to fear the consequences of getting into his car if he's under the influence of alcohol. And I want my fellow Americans to fear the results of living in a society that abandons its moral compass.

One of my healthy fears was that I wouldn't be the best parent possible when your Dad was born. I remembered what I experienced as a child, understood the psychology of parenting, and definitely was elated at the thought of doing things with my new son. Nevertheless, feelings of inadequacy, unworthiness, and anxiety can generate fear in the blink of an eye.

So without the benefit of having the perfect parenting manual as a resource, I decided that it might be helpful to reach out to some of my friends who had recently been new parents. I asked them for their input and advice as to what

I might experience in the coming months and how they managed similar situations. Of course, my friends were a wonderful source of encouragement and support, and my pre-parenting fears quickly disappeared.

For all of the situations that I've encountered in life concerning fear, either my own or someone else's, prayer has always been the foundation for the resources that I've used to manage that fear constructively.

And the payer that speaks most clearly to the remedy for fear in any situation from my perspective is Psalm 23 in the Old Testament of the Bible:

The Lord is my shepherd;
there is nothing I lack.
In green pastures you let me graze;
to safe waters you lead me;
you restore my strength.
You guide me along the right path
for the sake of your name.
Even when I walk through a dark valley.
I fear no harm for you are at my side;
your rod and staff give me courage.
You set a table before me
as my enemies watch;
You anoint my head with oil;
my cup overflows.
Only goodness and love will pursue me
all the days of my life;
I will dwell in the house of the Lord
for years to come.

Ethan, there will be many times in your life when unhealthy fears will be knocking at your door. When you sense that happening, always remember those three special gifts of intellect, emotions, and will that God has given you, and use them to restore your balance and direction in life. Finally, know that God is always with you. Make Psalm 23 your guide and trust that it will lead you along the right path.

I love you, Ethan.
Grandpa

"Miracles happen every day. Change
your perception of what a miracle is and
you'll see them all around you."

Jon Bon Jovi

EAR ETHAN:

Miracles happen in our world. I've seen my share of them
over the years. Your great-grandmother would say that my
life is a miracle since I died at birth and returned to life
thanks to the doctors and nurses who were there helping
me. When your Dad was born, I witnessed the miracle of
life, and when you came into the world, I saw that miracle
all over again.

I knew a fifteen-year-old girl who was cured from
cancer and a high school athlete's career-ending injuries
disappear on X-rays with no reasonable explanation from
the medical personnel who treated him. Verifiable stories of
profound healings have been plentiful in books, articles, and
religious and medical journals. Other miracles find people
surviving incredibly overwhelming and life-threatening
situations that defy all odds.

I researched the true story of a baby who was delivered prematurely by emergency cesarean to a wonderful couple, Margaret and Gary. It was a warm July night when their doctor entered the room to talk to them about their new son, Adam, who was twelve inches long and one pound, eight ounces in weight.

"I don't think he's going to make it," the doctor said. "There's only a 10 percent chance he will live through the night and even then, his future could be a very cruel one." He then went on to describe the problems that Adam could face, like never being able to walk or talk. He would most likely be blind and he could experience other catastrophic medical complications such as cerebral palsy or complete mental retardation.

For the next several days Adam desperately clung to life with all of the medical help that his tiny body could endure. Because of his underdeveloped nervous system, even the slightest kiss or caress was painful to him so his parents couldn't even comfort their own child or cradle him to their chests.

They asked God to stay close to their precious child, and as the weeks passed he slowly gained weight and strength. When he reached the two-month milestone, his mother was able to hold him in her arms. However, at five months the physicians were continuing to warn that Adam's chances for survival were still slim to none and living a normal life was next to impossible.

At four years old, Adam displayed no signs of mental

retardation and, other than being smaller, his feistiness more than made up for his size. If this was not sufficient for a miracle, it's far from the end of the story.

While Adam was sitting in his mother's lap one day watching his brothers ride their bicycles outside, in the midst of his endless chatter, he hugged his arms across his chest and asked, "Do you smell that?" Sensing an approaching thunderstorm, his mother replied, "Yes, it smells like rain."

Totally absorbed in the moment, Adam shook his head and patted his shoulders with his small hands and announced with great certainty, "No, it smells like Him. It smells like God when you lay your head on His chest."

Adam jumped down to play, as tears came to his mother's eyes. His words confirmed what Adam's parents had known all along: that during his first two months of life when his nerves were too sensitive to permit them to hold him, God was cradling Adam close to His chest and it was His loving scent that Adam now remembered so distinctly.

Not only do I believe that God causes miracles to happen in our world, but I also believe that since we're created in His image and likeness, an expectation of our lives is that we will make miracles happen as well.

In an earlier letter, I shared with you my belief that the real purpose of life is to know people, to engage people, and to uplift people. Whenever we bring joy, happiness, comfort, and peace to another, we enrich the miracle of life that God has given to us.

So my prayer for you, Ethan, is that you will always embrace and celebrate life as a miracle, knowing that you have already been a miracle to me.

I love you, Ethan.
Grandpa

About the Author

*T*OM MCQUEEN died shortly after he was born. Apparently God wasn't expecting such a quick trip home so He returned Tom to his parents, Joe and Marie McQueen.

The enlightenment of that journey from birth to death and back to life again permanently colored Tom's world as a Christian therapist, consultant to Fortune 500 companies, personal coach, and author. His inspirational workshops and seminars have touched the hearts of audiences throughout North America.

Tom is the president of the American Family Foundation, Inc., a not-for-profit organization whose mission is to enrich the lives of children and families in the United States.

An avid Tampa Bay Lightning hockey fan, Tom celebrates the blessings of his family, friends, and colleagues on Florida's beautiful west coast. And one of his very first gifts to Ethan was, of course, a miniature hockey stick.

Other Books by Tom McQueen

➢ Near-Life Experiences: Discovering New Powers for Personal Growth

> The Customer is WHY! Six Steps to Creating Legendary Service in Your Organization

> Passion at Work: Ten Things Legendary Leaders Do To Improve Performance, Productivity, & Profit

> BayCare Coaching: Helping Our Team Members Learn, Grow, and Develop

To order additional copies of *Letters to Ethan: A Grandfather's Legacy of Life and Love,* visit either: www.amazon.com or www.letterstoethan.com.

To schedule Tom for a speaking engagement, seminar, or workshop, contact the American Family Foundation at www.familyfoundation.us.

Have you ever thought about writing letters to your children or grandchildren as a lasting legacy?

Tom is starting a national campaign to encourage parents and grandparents to write letters to the next generation. Please visit: www.legacynationusa.com to read letters from others and to begin work on your legacy.